PINK POISON

A MEMOIR OF AN EATING DISORDER

To myself, from myself.

NICOLE LYNN

PROLOGUE

Brisking into the morning sunlight, I'm awaiting daybreak, what it holds. Has to offer for me. This repetitive motion followed by an elongation of self-inflicted torture that lasts for hours at a time continues into my early 20's waiting for that moment of redemption. I am who I am. This is me. Hatred masks over my eyelids as I stare in the mirror, disappointed again, no one to blame but myself. I grab every inch of unwanted mass that sits there on my body, laughing at me straight in the face telling me that I have lost, that there is no winning in this game.

I can feel it in my bones, the weakening feeling engulfing my limbs as I try to raise them up and down. It feels off to move my body parts. I feel dead as if the gravitational pull of the earth is asking for me to burry in its dirt. To consume another recycled soul into the ground awaiting decomposing bodies to turn into its soil once again. They put pretty girls in little boxes, right?

I've been away from home tired of the nonsense that fills my day-to-day life as an adolescent, not knowing which direction to take my life.

Right now, I exist in social problems. Right now, I need a way out of California. Runaway from the issues that swarm my mind with enticing thoughts of negativity and self-harm. Oh, yea and Anorexia's whispers sending me into a depression that only exists in my mind. Right now, I'm still lying in bed.

Pathetic,

Right now, I want to embody someone else. I've created an exhausting life that I can't keep up. Not on my own. That's where my Anorexia comes in as my alter ego. I fantasize about trading places with one of my idols, but that thought quickly fades because I don't have any.

Even more pathetic,

I stagger towards the bathroom look in the mirror. I can feel the mania build. I can feel the breakdown creep up into my consciousness. It's been waiting there since last night when my body was on autopilot gorging on glutinous items I tried so desperately to avoid. The guilt from gluttony always happens after a binge. I try to remember the context of last night's actions. I remember the lack of willpower. I remember trusting myself. Fucking idiot. I remember it started with space in my daily planner. I should have known better to fill in the blank spaces. I was at home. It was late at night after everyone had drifted into their bedrooms and fallen asleep.

I was lying in bed, my stomach gurgling trying to find substance in its emptiness. I couldn't stand the pain any longer. I went downstairs to find something to calm the hunger deep within me; I wish it didn't exist. When I walked into the kitchen, the cold tiles made the reality of my greed come alive because the kitchen is the only place cold to the barefoot touch. I looked up at the clock. 2 am, I can't remember the last time I had a good night's rest. I turned towards the cupboard frozen, just standing there. I don't know for how long, but it felt like ages. Softly I rested my hand on the doorknob like it was a delicate antique, but it wasn't because we live in a modern home. Part of me was scared of that doorknob. It signified a lack of control. Touching that doorknob made me feel weak and powerless, but the tiles made me think that way also. I want to blame the autopilot, but I can't. I have to take responsibility.

The door let out a soft creek as I opened it and startled my ears, giving me the slightest adrenaline rush. Then upon looking at the masses of prepackaged store-bought goods sent me over the edge. I slammed the door shut and stood frozen yet again. I stood there, thinking about all the boxes and cans that tainted my mind. All of a sudden, I swung the door back open gingerly, looking at everything placed on the shelves. Everything I have not allowed myself to consume since I started this diet. After seductively looking at every single product, I found myself holding the Jiff peanut butter jar. Grasping it in my left hand, I unscrew the vibrant red lid with my right. Instantaneously the kitchen was filled with that overpowering smell of creamy comfort. I tried to hold my breath, but I could already taste the delicious buttery spread on my taste buds. I raised the jar to my nose, thinking maybe if I inhale the scent, the craving would fade. I was wrong. The longing deepened; my mouth started slowly salivating for the light brown creamy lipid. The next thing I know is I'm upstairs again sitting on my bed with the television on, but it's just white noise. I'm not concentrated. My full-undivided attention is on this high of the spoon to jar to the jar to mouth. The silver spoon dives into a sea of peanuts and oil then find its way to my mouth. I'm smacking my lips together.

Throat dry from how quickly I am consuming my selfishness. No control. An hour has passed. I can finally see the transparency of the jar. I'm frantically scrapping the sides, bottom, and each crevice of the Jiff jar not wanting to let go. To let go of this binge, this feeling. There's no more. Done. The spoon falls slowly on the bed next to me, spreading its poison on my duvet. There is peanut butter dripping off the corners of my mouth. My throat is dry, and my lips are chapped. The room fills with the

intoxicating smell, and I have tainted my sanctuary once again.
16,000 calories of self-hatred

You know they say when learning psychology, the color red
makes you hungry. I try to calm myself down with that thought,
but you were already on the tiles and touching the doorknob,
weren't you. It wasn't the color you fat pig.

ANA

Beautiful creatures live inside my head. Perfect ones. The mind likes to think it's perfect. My mind wants to run away from trauma, that is. When bored, my brain can come up with the most absurd way to entertain itself. Body dysmorphia. Oh, it's so much fun. I am playing what it seems like a never-ending game of hide and seek with my eating disorder. Got a medical status of being unhealthy, I made the cut guys. Coming close to death having my doctors say they don't think I will make it. So close to the end, my parents started planning my funeral. Oh, yea, I'm not missing out on any fun in my youth.

Depression sets in every day of my life. Not living as one is supposed to but creating my world of torture and brutal violence. Making it to your goal weight than setting a new goal right away, nothing ever good enough. Never thin enough. Never. That's your mind, and you can't run away from suppressed emotion and thoughts no matter how much therapy you've received in your life.

Before I begin, let's catch you up on how the disease manifested into my life. Hmmm, let's see... growing up was alright. My family moved to a town called Cameron Park from San Meteo In California. My stepdad swept my mom off my feet. He took us far away from the city down a country road that led to a two-story home with a pool. Later the house was filled with puppies, friends, and memories. My mom had a new baby, and My older sister and I had a new sister. Then 2008 happened. My family filed for bankruptcy. There was more stress, more drinking, and even more arguments. Walking in on my mom face down in her own vomit was typical. So was my stepdad's absence. The energy in the house was enough to keep me away. I began competitive cheerleading and made new friends. I was never home. My mother used to call the cops on me to tell me to come home. They only found me a few times. Memories turned into blacked-out moments in time. My body started to do a new coping mechanism now that it was in constant fight or flight mode.

I left the mayhem to stay with my friend and her mom in Pismo Beach for the summer. I flourished! In the early hours of the morning, if mama K (my friend's mom) was still sleeping, we would skip out of the house, steal the car, and take off to buy the best cinnamon rolls known in town. We would get all dolled up and walk the beach to the pier every day to enjoy the creamiest clam chowder bread bowls. We would see who could get the darkest by baking our skin in the blaring sun, all of us lathered in baby oil. I was happy. I ate quite a large sum of the unhealthy fried foods and didn't think about a care in the world. That is until Mama k looked at me one day after a long period of silence she blurted out.

"Looking a little fat there, aren't we?"

I didn't react sourly. I was confused. Here was this 200 plus pound lady telling me I might've had one too many muffins. Ok. I brushed it off. The summer went by swimmingly, and it was coming to an end. I packed my suitcase, buttoned my shorts that fit a tiny bit snugger than the beginning of the summer, and boarded the Amtrak for Sacramento. When I arrived, my mom, who was waiting for me, had the biggest smile on her face. Mine mirrored hers. I missed her. We have always been close. Even if we're miles away mentally.

During my time in Pismo, my parents also lost the house. They moved into a townhouse down the street from where we used to live. My belongings had already been packed and placed in the new home, so it was just me that the room was missing. Perfect. I entered the unfamiliar structure that would be my new bedroom and sat down on the floor. Closed my eyes and drifted off to sleep. The next morning I came downstairs to find my stepdad cooking breakfast. The smells were intoxicating. I reached for something out of the fridge, and my stepdad turned around to say I had gained some weight, but it looked terrific on me. I panicked. I ran upstairs, jumped on the scale, and waited. 3, 2, 1,... BEEP 140 lbs. I immediately felt fat. I had to make a plan. With sweaty palms, I wrote down a diet and workout regime that I would stick to. Cheer had stopped over the summer, and I wasn't planning on enrolling this year. I decided it would be a good idea to take up the same conditioning that they made us do months before the competition. So that's what I did. As the months grew longer, so did my workouts. In 100 degree weather,

I would first saran wrap my thighs. Then thighs and waist. That eventually turned into wrapping my whole body and then covering up in layers of clothing on top of it. Three miles turned into ten.

I started to become afraid of food. I would fast for a consecutive three days and end it accidentally binging and gaining some weight back. This went on for a while. Three days of fasting turned in fourteen. A cookie for a binge ended up being the entire kitchen. I was stealing money from my mom to pay for my habits. My thinking started to become irrational. My depression worsened. I was in an argument with my mom and blurted out that I hadn't eaten in weeks. Silence.

The next morning I was taken to my doctor. I only just got my mouth open when my mom started breaking out in hysterics, telling the doctor of all the habits of mine she has observed and what I told her. I was checked up and referred to an intensive eating disorder outpatient facility in Sacramento, CA. 3 hours a day, 5 days a week turned into 3 hours a day, 3 days a week. I played their game. I graduated from group therapy and the program. I started working out again. Harder.

A few months later, I was back in the grips of my eating disorder. The fights in the family home got worse. So did my depression. I was contemplating what I could do to help myself. I thought of my Whidby Island family, I always have a good time there. Maybe I just need a break from Cameron Park. I convinced my mom to buy me a ticket. I told her that the trip would help my stress levels and hers too. I told her that I was going to be in good hands and well-watched after. She believed me. She trusted me. However, she just didn't know I wasn't ready.

WASHINGTON

I made it to Washington to escape the never-ending carnage that inherits my thought process; I just wanted to get away to see if the pain would stop. A two-week-long period of freedom from something, nothing? I don't even know, but I know that I was depressed and a burden to my family. I needed to get away. My family in Washington is full of life adventures and excitement, turning every day into one for the books. Their routine consisted of arising with the sun and enjoying every moment until past the time the sun dissipates. Every day was full of activities, hiking, kayaking, tennis, and swimming. There were parties and gatherings every night. Arriving in their home with warm welcomes and comfort made me tender. With ease, I settled in the motions of their lives as if I had been there all along, but it wasn't enough, it's never enough. I can feel it, I'm losing my strength, but I didn't have enough mental energy to stop.

"no, nothing to eat for breakfast, but I'll have some coffee, oh no, no soy milk or sugar, black please, thanks," I say thank you way too much. Still, I can't help it; it's a people-pleasing quality that's been integrated into my personality, making me the creature I am.

After my morning coffee, I would start on a morning walk adventuring down into town. Langley, the small town that my aunt and uncle resided in, was breathtaking. Green for miles. The hue of the color making it as if you were in a motion picture. Nature overtook this small town; the storms made sure it never turned brown. Still, most of the time, that meant the days were grey.

Grey days became depressing, eventually. Walking around the town and venturing into the woods was my first attempt at getting away from that depression. It was the only time I felt like I wasn't critiquing myself. I was absorbing everything around me as a child does when it first learns to do everyday tasks. Trying to find simplicity in life and enjoying it for being real and beautiful. I found myself walking along the beach, only to realize that finding enjoyment in my time was spent wandering around burning calories. My eating disorder decided to show up. Actually, it was probably always here with me. I thought I had left it at home, but you can't run away from yourself. My eating disorder thoughts grew louder and louder, commanding me to go keep burning calories, keep exploring, and I did. At first, it was exciting; the beach I was on led me to a dirt trail. The trail became longer more exciting and led to different avenues of wildlife and terrain. The path took me through the woods where the trees were hundreds of years old, and each tree that grew higher could tell a thousand tales of people, places, and time. The woods lead me through to another beach where the ocean waves engulfed my eardrums as the crashing sea sent waves of serenity through me. The sand took me to an urban surrounding where only the world and I existed. My feet melting into its funky grains like a hug from a mother comforting its child. Only then did I get a chance to slow down enough. Those feelings would fade daily into the night, taking me back to houses, homes, and the television blaring with socialites.

While everyone tiptoed off to sleep, insomnia joined me on the couch to watch time pass until Anorexia wanted to take control.

No matter how warm and welcome I felt in my aunt and uncle's home, my ED was there to warn me that it wasn't enough as it crept up on me. When thoughts of hunger could not reside any longer. At night after not eating all day, anxiety-ridden, and in a house where everyone is sleeping, my appetite started to get greedy. Cells took over. My brain shut off. The vital part of my starving body wafted me into the kitchen, where I would cook and eat gorging on anything the glutinous side of me wanted.

Brownies were in the oven rising slowly with double chocolate chips that melted delicately into the mixture while climbing in the oven. While the brownies were baking, I cooked spinach pasta. Ripping the bag open with my teeth. Flying the triangle squares onto the frying pan, spicing them in oregano dousing them with generous tablespoons of olive oil. I'm now salivating to the intoxicating smells of the delicious cuisines I had been frantically making. Not patient enough to await the food, I had taken up the stovetop and counter space and began at the cupboards to find some ready to eat foods. I shoveled spoonful after spoonful of cereal down my throat. Ripping the roof of my mouth to shreds by the harsh granola cereal, not soggy enough to treat my mouth with kindness, just like my greed.

Soy milk dripping down my face while the gravity pulled it onto my clothing and puddled it onto the floor. Reminding me later of my actions no matter how hard I want to forget, every single time I lose control. Crackers stuffed greedily down my throat. Sometimes swallowing cracker bits whole. That also left my mouth with scars from how forceful the binge episode was. Creamy peanut butter by the spoonful smeared on top of the freshly made brownies that were almost too gooey at times. Not baked in the oven long enough because of how impatient my stomach was aching for more food screaming at me. My stomach was screaming to feed it more and never satisfied. Not stopping to care food had me in a trance back to the cupboards for more where after I had felt so sick, you could mistake me for being pregnant. Unopened boxes would be left empty on the side of the trash the next day and hopefully not found missing to make me feel guilty about last night's wrongdoings. Of everything Anorexia, and I have worked for. I would then have realized what had happened. I would feel shame and guilt to the extent where I couldn't handle who I had become for the last few hours of the night. Ashamed. Always ashamed.

I am creeping down the hallway now, making sure no one was up that I haven't woken anyone up with the loud crashing and banging and box opening. Or crumpling of the synthetic plastic material that keeps it from rotting in the shelves of grocery stores. The noise that takes place when you're tearing the kitchen to shreds. I make it down the hallway to the bathroom and turn the shower on, pull back my hair, and stick my fingers down my throat. Not satisfied until I'm vomiting bile and blood, or pass out from exhaustion.

During the night, I would clean up the mess that I made during the binge episode and cautiously write down things I needed to get at the store. I've tainted the atmosphere, and I'm even more depressed. I hardly sleep just to be engulfed in the morning sun and living off Anorexia's script of what to say and how to act I desperately want this vacation to end. It didn't help. It made things spiral. I cried myself to sleep that night. Feeling lonely in a place where I thought the loneliness would fade, I realized that my setting wasn't the problem, I continuously am the problem.

There's no escaping yourself, no running or hiding from yourself either. With the days getting longer and the hours being more excruciating than the last, I called my mom and begged her to help me with a plane tick home early. I told her that I tried to flee the depression by running away from my situation back home, but the negative thoughts just packed their bags and came with me. She agreed to help me, and the next day I was off again.

Washington was now coming to an end, and all I had been doing for the past week was self destruct.

Get up

Shower

Breakfast (black coffee)

10-mile hike

snack (apple)

Hang out with the family

Watch House on TV until everyone falls asleep around 11pm

binge, purge, shower

pray for sleep. I was falling apart

HOME AGAIN

I landed in Sacramento and was immediately welcomed by the dry heat. Scurrying off the plane and headed for baggage claim, I spotted my mom. On the way down the escalator, I could see her standing anxiously.

There it was, that same familiar stare, that's what I call the checklist stare. That also came with a similar checklist hug my mom, and I got into on occasion. I couldn't even appreciate that hug because the embrace came with a pretense, checking for bones. I was so used to the stares, the silent gasps coming from across the room. They were almost like compliments. The last time I stepped on the scale, it said 79 pounds, I was thin, but my eating disorder told me I wasn't small enough. As we drove home, I thought of all the new outfits I could feel good in now. I was thin enough to feel comfortable. I was tired enough not to have the racing thoughts of "you're not good enough. Keep going, you're pathetic. There's plenty of girls out there thinner than you why so you deserve a break from working out and looking good, looking good is a reward, and you haven't earned it yet." Not allowing myself to enjoy food and rest turned into not deserving compliments and friendships. I was often depressed and on a synthetic high from my eating disorder. I was lonely from everyone running away, being too scared to still be my friend. Afraid of my skeletal frame and unhinged temper. It didn't bother me that badly. I was already used to not having enough time to fit in social activities anyway. Does anyone know how much time it takes to stay that thin?

Each workout regimen an hour longer than the previous day anorexia became my full-time job. Anorexia's pressuring voice growing louder with each pound lost. Each meal skipped; she stripped my identity. All I could manage anymore was a non-genuine hello, and a somewhat half blissful smile plastered over the remains of who I used to be. Only to find myself seconds later in the indifferent state of mind, I wallow around with observing things and not talking much. That was the new me. No one understood that it's just easier that way; they don't know;

they never will. What happened to Nicole they ask, don't question it's easier to pretend not to be curious.

We pulled into the driveway, my anxiety started spiking. My heart rate quickly climbed, and beads of sweat started pilling on my forehead. I try and calm myself down with the thoughts of I'm safe tonight. Mom won't discuss the way I look to my face, I know Mom won't make a scene at least not in public, not when she's mentally unprepared. However, that safe feeling didn't last long. Minutes after we arrived home, I could sense her masking a plan. Her silent stares and exaggerated sighs. I could hear her whispering on the phone with Kaiser how to get me into the EDIOP (eating disorder intensive outpatient program) as soon as she could. However, my flight arrived late. Kaiser's offices were closed at this hour, and mom wanted to take me straight there for a "check-up," but since the offices were closed for the evening, my panic subsided.

Until the next morning, my mom spent all morning rushing to take me to this therapy appointment. I didn't fight it. I slumped into the car layered in tights, leggings, jeans, a tee-shirt, a crew neck, and a hoodie. 100-degree heat in the middle of summer, and I was still cold.

Dancing with this disease for as long as I have people don't understand the distraught behind the thinness, they bypass it as a modelesque fad, something the waif will get over with time. Only to discover it's not a phase. It's a life of pretending and internalizing and being an actress. In our family, having a bad day didn't exist outside the home. It just didn't, so we were all outstanding actors. Picture perfect. How are you? Good. How's everything? Great! That's just the way it is.

That's how I was expecting to doctor visit to go. I could just plaster my counterfeit smile and attitude for a few minutes while I tell my story so I can get back with my ways. I stepped out of the car onto the blinding new black asphalt of the Kaiser hospital parking lot and watched my mother from my peripherals follow me inside the doors. She stayed behind me more nowadays never to lose sight of her little girl, I assume. Walking in the familiar sterile sent infected my nose. I bypass the fumes of the hospital nonchalantly. I have been here way too many times that I can hardly detect any hospital smell at all. I spend so much time at the hospital that everywhere else is messy and smells horrible even if it doesn't. We check-in, sit down, and are called within a few minutes. Coet the therapist covering for my usual therapist, Liss, calls me in. I guess my therapist was on vacation and didn't feel the need to inform me, or maybe it was the fact that I had been with Liss for three years already, and nothing had changed.

First things are first mini-physical. Coet firmly handed me a paper-thin gown to change into before getting on the scale. I used to add more weight to my body by hiding ankle weights in my bra. Five pounds could make or break your progress and send you home or to inpatient treatment. Water loading always helped too, but I didn't have the energy to care about those little things anymore. I was sent to the restroom to do a urinalysis (UA). The liquid content in the cup was reddish-brown for how much body was eating itself. Ketosis (a metabolic state in which the body feeds off its own fat cells to receive nourish). I should've seen this as a negative sign, but again I just didn't have the means to care. I came out to Coet's office then was told where I was going.

The plan, already set. Paperwork, done. Still being an adolescent, there wasn't anything I could say or do to convince them that I was stable. I tried to convince myself that I was stable, and my mind believed my lies, but my body was sending help signals. Like I had a choice in going anyway because there I was. No hiding from anyone anymore. Visibly frail. I relapsed hard, and I was too weak to come up with any more excuses. I was 51/50ed. I fully believed that getting admitted to the hospital under medical advice was a goal I had to achieve to be anorexic.

I didn't think I was thin enough for that honor. I didn't find them funny, me anorexic? Maybe I didn't eat enough, but no, I wasn't anorexic. No, first of all, I was not thin enough even though I was a mere 79 lbs. Now, nine pounds too heavy, I thought not quite there yet. Sure I was dizzy, tired, weak, but wasn't every adult? I couldn't see myself withering away because of body dysmorphia. I didn't see a bone protruding frame. I didn't see skin stretched over muscles and veins. I saw the pudge on my stomach. I saw the fat on my upper arms, the thigh gap not wide enough. Someone had to intervene before I got to the finish line. Before I lost the game for good.

51/50

"She's frail" I overheard them talking about me, someone's always talking about me these days. "We have to stabilize her before she leaves." I was half proud of myself for achieving the hollowed-out figure I've become. Half disappointed that it's being taken away from me and seldom thinking I want to be saved but also too tired to care. Too tired to care about anything these days, shifting to make to body sores go away from flesh sitting stagnant in one place for too long. Too feeble, too tired even so that when Coet told me I would die from this disease, I thought she was being overdramatic and exaggerating a bit.

Blood work doesn't lie. It said I was dying, slowly. I felt it with every inhale and exhale. Every next one shorter and farther in between. My body yawning more frequently to expand my rib cage and provide more sips of oxygen to my lungs, I was dying, and I was the only one ok with that. "Nicole, are you listening? We're leaving now" the nurses and EMTs were alert. I had no choice, too into my thoughts to notice more hot tears that have streamed down either side of my cheeks. Quickly I adapted to my surroundings and came back to reality. I was 51/50ed because I was harmful to myself and a threat to my life. Right now, secured to the gurney, they wheeled me into the back of the ambulance. My mind drifted off on how I ended up here and why maybe something will make sense this time. I was first being admitted to the Kaiser pediatric center in Roseville, CA because my body was not stable enough to be exposed directly to inpatient. My heart rate was too low. My heart muscle was shrinking; I wasn't allowed to sleep at night because it was dropping to below 30 beats per minute. I was the living dead, and inpatient can't take someone at risk of dying because of their liabilities and policies. I think they don't want families to sue.

We arrived at the medical hospital in Roseville, CA. The EMTs strapped me down and wheeled me out. I was silent. I was escorted out of the gurney to a small office to do assessments and admissions. I felt defeated. The fluorescent lights blinded me, making me synthetically tired as they always do. I finished the paperwork in a matter of hours and was taken out to the hallway. To my surprise, there was a wheelchair with a nurse staring at me. I looked behind me to see if someone was standing there. There wasn't. He was staring at me. I had to get in that thing? No way. I tried to argue my way out of it, but maybe I should've spent 3 hours filling out the paperwork instead of skimming. I just handed my life over, literally. I had to follow their rules. So In an angry attempt, I tried to make the nurse as uncomfortable as possible by being a total bitch. It only made me feel lonelier.

ED

You don't wake up one morning and decide you're going to have an eating disorder. You don't dream of starving yourself. No one grows up wanting to become the person that eats food only to have it come back up ten minutes later in the bathroom, but somehow I got there.

I don't know where my story starts, and I don't think I'll ever really know. I don't know if my eating disorder has been waiting on the sidelines to approach me when the disease thought the time was right. Ready to confidently come into my life, to change my ways. I know that I was innocent, in an unknown venerable state of mind while other peers around me strived to be the characters they once thought were their heroes.

We all grew up to find out heroes don't exist. The disease mimicked all the kids who used to bully me in school. It repetitively made negative side comments to me whenever I was triggered. I listened to it, and those thoughts were so

monotonous its what became permanent. I started repeating all
the hateful things said to me in my head. I couldn't get the cycle
of violence out of my thoughts.

My thought process is severely black and white, so when I
wanted to do something, it was all or nothing. Someone
commented that I was fat; I just stopped eating. I knew if I
started my old competitive cheer conditioning, I would get back
into shape, no problem. I thought by treating myself strictly, I
would reach the goal quickly. I didn't realize that doing so came
with learning how to hate yourself. I didn't think the thoughts
would become perpetual. I never thought I would be afraid to eat
food, but over time I became terrified. Over time I hated
everything about myself more and more. I continued to treat
myself with hate for so many years achieved becoming
emaciated. I didn't want to be me anymore. I wasn't.

My eating disorder was also probably a recipe made up of sexual
abuse, having a best friend that had bulimia binge-purge
subtype, and previously being in competitive sports. Flashbacks
of negativity would flood my mind while I was sitting stagnant.

There was no way to turn off the noise, but the continuous opposing demands I was creating managed to do the job. Flashbacks of what I could not control in my current life kept flashbacks from childhood away. My childhood is a blank screen. I can only piece it together with photographs. Memories were taken away from me from my brain and stored in the very depth where I cannot find them any longer. There was too much bad, so my brain sacrificed my memories for my sanity. This cycle of my brain storing negative memories occurred so much that by the time I was a teenager, it started appearing in forms of disorders, like running and restricting.

My clinical diagnosis is anorexia nervosa, severe depression, OCD (obsessive-compulsive disorder), and OCPD obsessive-compulsive personality disorder. That is what is keeping my mind busy, so I don't have to think about my childhood abuse.

My eating disorder has not only become my best friend, my worst enemy, my nightmare. My sickness is now the majority of my identity. I didn't want to lose my eating disorder for this reason, who would I be if I wasn't the fit girl. I didn't want to miss the integrity I created, but it was sending me to the grave, so I have to try my hardest to let it go.

ADMISSION

We arrived at the Kaiser pediatrics hospital in Roseville. I was
not well enough to be admitted to the inpatient ward. The nurses
said something like I wasn't medically stable enough. I thought
they were the ones delirious. I felt fine. I was removed from the
gurney to a wheelchair because walking was considered too much
energy wasted from my body, I tried to walk the paramedic
caught me and shoved me back down by my shoulders, I guess I
am sitting in this whether I like it or not. "No different than last
time," I muttered to myself. We wheeled into the front office
were the ambulance party left us, and my mother and I were left
to wait. Then we were escorted into the admissions office. I was
probed with a serious of questions, thinking to myself this is the
part where they define if I'm crazy or not? After the psych
evaluation, a room number was assigned to me, and we left to
find it. Still chained to the wheelchair, I was like a helpless child
pushed to my room. Arriving on the floor, I heard everything. I
closed my eyes and listened to the papers shifting in the Nurses'

hands. I heard the soft sobs from other patient's rooms probably coming from worried family members caring about their loved ones when there's not much anyone can do to help. I heard time click by on the clocks determining our fate and existence in the world, and I heard myself for the first time in a while.

We entered the room. The nurse helped me from my wheelchair to bed. Then she asked me to change into the paper gown provided. She made me go to the bathroom in a bedside commode, and then I was weighed backward. Then the nurse filled a handful of glass vials with my blood and walked out of the room. Left with a bloody cotton ball, and my thoughts, the reality started to set in. The truth brought tears. I wept, I wept so hard that I was almost excited about how many calories I was burning by weeping. The bloodhound nurse came swiftly back into the room and attached me to new bags for my IV's. My body needed hydration. After 8 liters of fluid, my body was satisfied.

To avoid a feeding tube down my throat, I drank the ensures nurses were force-feeding me. Ensures are canned liquid meals that are high in caloric value. When the nurse came with the

ensure, if she gave it to you room temperature, it was nasty. If
you buddied up with nurses, as I did with some of them, went the
extra mile for you. My nurses would make ensure frosties for me
by dumping the can of vanilla or chocolate ensure into a
styrofoam cup and allowing it to freeze for a while before I had
to drink it. I am to drink them every three hours, from 8 am to 11
pm. I was used to nothing all day everyday besides the occasional
snack here and there. If anyone as an eating disorder patient
refused to drink the ensures the RN's would hunt you down a
stick a feeding tube up your nose and down your throat. Nurses
made you sit on the edge of the bed to eat your meals. They
wanted to make sure you didn't use tactics strategically used in
the past like spilling ensure down the bed sheets while the
nurses turned their heads or something adjacent to that. It also
had to be down your stomach in 30 minutes. Or you get the tube.
Every night I was awakened by nurses and loud buzzers coming
from my heart monitor, the machine told me to wake up because
my heart dipped to low while I was sleeping. It was confirming
that I was slowly committing suicide. I would look up at the
monitor and see my heart surviving on 35 beats per minute.
However, the nightly wake ups only lasted for three nights. The

35 BPM turned into 50, then 60 eventually gaining strength.
During the day, the nurses would wake me up at 6 am take my
blood and leave me until 8 am where I get handed my first shake
of the day. After forcefully drinking the toxic mixture, I am laid
to bed rest all day until each time I have to have an ensure or use
the bedside commode to use the bathroom. So, of course, I try to
take advantage of all the time drinking the ensures to invite
change in this never-ending routine of accumulating bedsores.
That is what happens day to day repetitively for seven days
beside the occasional family time. Seven harrowing days passed
bedridden and blank. That's when the doctor came in to tell me
the news. Alta bates called, they have your bed ready. Here we go
again.

HOSPITAL

I woke up to the paramedic, shifting my body around, "we're here." Alta bates the medical center in Berkley, CA. I was transferred by ambulance from the temporary placement at Kaiser. It's a shame. I was starting to like to be bedridden. Going from the Kaiser hospital to Alta bates meant an educated 24-hour watch, no one to trick because they knew all your tricks and played this game for a while. You're just one of the four jokers in the deck of cards. Let's pray this new doctor is an ace because they've all been jacks, and you're still dying. I want to scream to the doctor, "please help me out of this sorrow. If this is life, I'm tired of pretending to live human. How do you live correctly after seeing, feeling, and experiencing the psychological and physical state of where I have been. Life and reality don't connect anymore!" but I keep my mouth shut. It's easier not to figure out the equation, right? So, I'll slowly evaporate from it. It's hard being a curious person, and, for me, the thoughts never end. Neither do the questions.

I didn't receive a chance to pack any of my things to take with me to Alta bates in, so my mother grabbed what she could from the house and drove to meet us at the Berkeley ward. Since I was arriving from another hospital, all I had to do was check-in and arrive. Thankfully they transferred all of my paperwork because I didn't have to do all the initial admission nonsense you have to go through when you first arrive at the inpatient ward. Immediately after admission, I was escorted to my temporary room to be searched by a nurse from head to toe. My bags are thoroughly inspected and patted down before you can get the okay to leave the room. The nurse proceeded with removing my shoelaces and strings from my hoodies and stowed them away. Then she informs me I will not get them back until I discharge from the program. No makeup is allowed, and all of your grooming belongings are placed in a plastic tub locked away behind the nurse's station for safekeeping. After all the processing, the nurse took my vitals and showed me my room. Two twin beds covered in white, the purest of all colors and one single pillow, a substantial separate window is looking at a small courtyard with 1" thick, unbreakable glass protecting the actual lens and us from ourselves. There was also a bathroom. It had a toilet, sink, shower, and pathetic mini piece of metal bolted to the wall that was supposed to be our mirror. They didn't want the eating disordered body checking. Too bad we were too smart for that. The smart ones knew that when the sun went down at night, you could turn on your light and create a mirror in the window with the reflection of the glass, no one ever shared that secret I'm sure that's probably why the hospital still has windows I'm sure if they found out someone was doing so, they would board them up.

I set my things on top of the petite bed, said goodbye to my mother, who was waiting. I promised her I'd try my best and followed the nurse into a more massive hallway where my mother went right, and I went left. Hopefully, that was the ending of the worry that she burdened around with her because I was in better hands. I was safe now. I am then led to a room where a small group was sitting, walking over I felt the eyes size me up and down. They all looked at me, and whether they showed interest in getting to know me or not, all stared. I stared back. I didn't care if their gaze met mine. Some patients were overweight; some were underweight; some were average. Not everyone on the 3 East B ward was for eating disorder treatment. It was also a 51/50 ward for suicide attempts, personality disorders, and other causes of PTSD. I was just in time for dinner...great. First night and already shoveling crap down my esophagus. I half expected this to happen because I have been here before, but since this place has seen patients for only weeks at a time and years in between, we all come back, and they all remember who we are.

The Eating disorder patients or ED's taken to a table where one of the LVNs (Licensed Vocational Nurse) or nurses sit with us to watch our every move, you never know when someone could be stuffing food in their shirts or pant pockets. Sweaters and jackets? Not permitted at the dining table because of how many times patients tried to put food up their sleeves. The night shift nurse prepares my dinner for me. Infectious nutrients made up of greasy ground beef, a giant scoop of thick sour cream, pre-packaged shredded cheese, and a hard shell. It's taco night. I sit stagnant for a while until I have enough willpower to pick up the hard corn shell. I immediately feel the rush of anxiety and purposefully break the taco making a mess and making it look like an accident. The nurse doesn't take any crap, she tells me to try and eat the food and threatens me with an ensure, and no way am I consuming that shake again as it would quite possibly make me sick unwillingly because of the amount I had been absorbing for the past seven days. I cordially get away with just a few bites for dinner and a sour attitude. We can't leave the table until everyone has finished, and it's almost impossible to get a chance to leave the table before the allotted time given for main meals which are a half-hour and snacks which is fifteen minutes. After the disordered eating patients have finished, we're sent to line of sight in the day room for a half an hour before we all call it a night and go to bed. I can already tell I'll be up retracing my life over and over again, wondering where I went wrong.

MIDNIGHT THOUGHTS

No one wants this, but some end up like me stuck, scared, and alone. However, I do remember a time when I didn't have a daily goal in mind. The scale didn't reflect how I felt for the rest of the day, continually determining the intake and output. I laughed a lot and had a lot of friends. I spent the night at other people's houses. I was never at my house at all. My mother used to call the police to track my car just to make sure I came home for a couple of days or a week or something like that just so settle her mind, I'm assuming. Before my illness, I never wanted to be home. Friends were my life. I was utterly extroverted and in love with everything and anything around me. I wasn't introverted until my eating disorder manifested.

Why can't I be both people? Why can't I ever find the balance between wanting to go out and wanting to stay recluse? I only remember becoming reclusive after my first hospital stay when I had gained back all the weight I had lost, and trying to get rid of it again became my favorite pass time hobby. No more dinner with friends as I avoided food at all costs and didn't want to exploit my anorexic tactics to my peer friends because I was afraid of getting called out on my habits. Everyone found out about my disorder eventually. I couldn't hide my frail appearance any longer with oversized clothing because XXS and double zeros swallowed me. That was the first time that I stayed at Alta Bates.

After the first hospital admission, after gorging on all that food, consuming ten thousand calories in one day became my regular. I was shoved out of Alta Bates without proper examples of normalizing portion sizes, adequate therapy, or tools to stop anorexia from coming back into my life. I left going home knowing I would immediately relapse. I couldn't control the position my mindset was in, my disorder became greedy and hollowed out my thoughts to nothing but images of food and ridding of the extra waste I saw overtaking my body. I was a stranger to myself. I looked in the mirror and didn't recognize who was staring back. I heard Ana's whispers once again. I immediately started on my journey of lonesome tiring workouts and starvation.

Funny how that when I relapsed, I heard different demanding thoughts. New types of eating disorder thoughts that whisper sweet nothings into my ear, filling me with nonsense. It's a voice. It could be the way you give yourself positive or negative affirmations. It could be your voice of reason. I mean, we all have one. Your subconscious view is that view we didn't have control over, but it is the voice that tells you what to decide if given options. Say, for example, when you're at dinner sometimes you say to yourself hmmm better not have dessert tonight or perhaps, I should have fruit instead of chocolate. It's those kinds of thoughts we think to ourselves all the time to find guidance, sanity, or justification, maybe. In my case, to be perfect.

Perhaps it's just instinct, and the priorities have changed. If you think about it, we live in a pretty screwed up world ruled by people telling us what we want, what we should eat, and how to act, tempted with advertisements' subconscious drilling, magazine diets. She's too fat then she's too thin.

I look at the clock, midnight. I let the eyes roll back behind my head to stop the progressive thoughts. My blood feels thick. I can feel the toxic buildup of my life piling up on me, draining the means of my existence. I took sleeping pills tonight. Surely I would induce sleep to hide away from reality, the awkwardness of living, and the stale air others seem to linger behind invading in your space, forcing you to soak up its overwhelming energy. Tossing and turning, I give up and make my way towards the bathroom. I grip each side of the sink and try hard to find my reflection in the mirror. Pathetic excuses, tired skin, aging eyes are all I see as I stare myself in the mirror. I clench my eyes shut, trying to forget who I am, but nothing changes. I blink as hard as I can wishing I could finally wake up from this dream, but when I flutter my eyes open, I'm in the same place surrounded by the same shit. It doesn't go away; it never does. Get used to it darling, the cycles never going to change.

FLOORPLAN

The next morning, I woke up to the trembling ice-cold fingers the
night shift nurse had then a quick pinch from a needle that woke
me up indefinitely. I looked up towards the clock, not even 6 am,
and I'm already paying dues. It's my second day, but I should've
expected this kind of treatment from them. The policies never
change around here. After the RN takes my blood, I'm left sitting
another 2 hours before we have to get up for meds and morning
check-in. I try and write in my journal. I draw a blank. With
empty thoughts, I stagger towards the window and sit on the
ledge. Gazing out, I see a bird and am envious of this bird, it's
the ability to live and survive and not complicate things. Its
ability to just have nerve endings and not much thought process.
I must have stared out the window for ages because it felt as if I
only turned my head away for a moment as my thoughts were
distracted by shuffling noises coming from the hall. I peeked my
head around the corner. Transitory residents were receiving
their morning products in plastic boxes behind the nurse's

station like shampoo, conditioner, and soap. I go to retrieve my plastic tub from the nurse's station. We're not allowed to have any of our toiletries with us because the nurses caught one too many inpatients getting drunk off of Listerine, cutting themselves with razors, and other mentionable things. I shower and get ready even though I feel like it's pointless getting prepared here, but I have to play along if I want to get out.

Vitals were also a choice to take at this hour before they become mandatory after our allotted morning hygiene hour. I being a procrastinator, opted out for receiving my bathroom needs, and ran for the shower. The water doesn't stay hot for long, so you have the lather up run the water then water off repeat. I look down. Tears emerge, a bump the size of two fists sit where flat abs once were. "It was that damn dinner last night" The negative thoughts are back, "at least it's not Wednesday, and they didn't weigh you, you've probably gained, you'll never be perfect." Thanks for the confidence boost ED, tears roll down my face. I'm sulking in my sorrow with nothing to do, so I start repetitively punching myself in the stomach. I hit myself enough times where it's going to show later in colors of dark purple and blue, but I don't care as long as it shuts down my mind. Wherever the negative thoughts surface, I'll be black and blue all over if it gives me some quiet. I finish up getting ready for the day and head out for vitals. My blood pressure sucks, not a surprise, and I enter the day room where Andii, the med nurse, is handing out the doctor's orders.

The doctor prescribes each of us enough medication to keep us cold and hollow enough to narrow us down to just a number. We no longer have jurisdiction. We all try and drown ourselves in the numbing sedatives and stimulants before heading out to meet our fears face to face, aka food—the nourishment of life. Andii hands me my cup of drugs that were prescribed to me last time I was here. I glance down at the contents in the little white paper cup. Multivitamins for nutrition and Ativan, to sedate my emotions. "How are you? Didn't think we'd see you around here again" Andii openly comments, "um fine, I guess" is all I could manage. I took the pills, and anxiously waited for the Ativan to kick in. I know it won't take long. While I'm waiting for the drugs to kick in, the memories from my last stay start to surface. There is not too much to the place.

The dining hall is attached to the day room. It looks like a junk hall. A place where worn-down carpet and tiles are the only real identifications of where the rooms start and end. Besides the plastic furniture, it looks like the hospital went thrift shopping. They needed more government money. It's a disaster of a setup. You know if they're going to stick us all in confinement for a little, you would think they would care to spruce up the place a bit. Hence why I encourage residential like Remuda Ranch or Cielo House something that sounds pleasant where you can at least walk around outside. We get the pleasure of patio with thick 3-inch glass walls bordering is off, so we can't bother the ordinary people walking around. If your fates as worse as ours who need help, do the research first.

Pray every night you don't experience these adventures made for the game of loss and misery. Reality becomes hell, and all you want to do is escape, but everything you do to try and leave is messy. Cut not deep enough to penetrate the vein, pills one to short of poisoning the body to death. Gods keeping me alive, his reminder that there is an end to this hell, but if you can't survive the patience, you can doom yourself for eternity. Sometimes I feel like I would do better in another life. Well, I do believe in life after I don't know what it is, to think we are the only energies in the universe would be such a small thought.

Anyways back to the mundane tour, on the patio, there are brittle plastic chairs, some pottery with plants, and a basketball hoop. That's all that's out there. A few rustic items and yet again the adjacent wall a giant 3" thick glass wall held by cement pillars keeping us in but teasing us with its ability to been seen through by its transparency. So, we continue into the kitchen where there are about 6 square tables. To the left of our "grand" dining room set up is a kitchen island. On Saturdays, the island holds the trays of food they send-up from downstairs when we get cooked meals and don't get the pre-portioned out hospital rubbish they send-up. Beyond the kitchen island, there is a fridge with a padlock on the freezer and fridge door, so we don't binge and purge our feelings away. Welcome to 3 East B, where the eating disordered, depressed suicide attempters, and mentally unstable unite.

ROUTINE

In the morning, I can't sleep, so I write: Uneven energy settles in as I hear broken records continually playing in the background of my routine world that I can't escape. I am trying so hard, but no one understands how difficult it is to try as hard as I have. Years have gone by, and I wish the long strides it takes to climb mountains would end, I don't know how much longer my muscles can keep up. Even resting in the dream world seems impossible when all you ever do is have nightmares. Cold sweats wake you up from the only place you feel safe, and you're not safe anywhere. I wonder why this is happening to me and why I always feel like I'm climbing, I can never rest, and now I'm starting not even to have enough energy to ask anymore. It seems like I have already been waiting a lifetime to figure it out, but I probably will never get an answer. I'm on the path to recovery from an anorexia nervosa. I have been living with this monster for ten years now. Ten years of self-induced torture and hatred. Ten years of triple-checking my thoughts and actions, overthinking, caring too much. It leads to a state of exhaustion that no one living in the normie world will ever know.

I drop the pen, proud of myself for writing again.

When it's time to start the scheduled day, which happens to be 8:00 am, we're shouted out into the day room to await our first major obstacle, breakfast.

The trays are not here yet. We are left to roam the day room alone, and everyone was already out in the halls, so I brace myself for anything I'm about to experience. I walk out into the Dayroom and see a few people, mostly girls, but there is a boy. I come out to the sad space of existence and immediately turn back to my bedroom to wait for breakfast. Sitting in there probably won't be as bad as all the size ups or awkward introductions I thought to myself. I tried to step back towards my room, but my mind was just too curious. I turned around again and again, and again, pacing. This happens so much sometimes. I'm deciding back and forth talking to myself it looks like I'm some crazy person, but I catch that I'm doing it quickly and stop. I take a deep breath, hold it in, and wait for an answer. I'm going in the Dayroom, that's it, no changing your mind you are doing it!! As I walk, I think of things I saw earlier to distract myself, so I'm not just an aloof walking around the Dayroom by myself looking like a complete idiot who doesn't know what she's doing. I remember the food chart on the wall that'll be sure to keep me busy and to keep me away from awkward introductions or staredowns between other patients. I walk towards it.

The diagram on the wall will contain what will be eating for each meal each day, seven days a week. It controls any eating disorder patient that comes in and out through those double doors that make you feel like a victim in your years of youth. I remember looking at it and thinking okay there's a lot of food here, but it's not as much as I binged before in one sitting, little did I know in the coming days my meal plan would be four times the size of the written one on the chart. Finally, it was time. We all sat down at the table closest to the double doors. It was a bad idea because it was a reminder that we were stuck here. We were held obeying the rules and eating their food and away from our family and friends. Maybe we're placed here because we have to re-find who we are as a result of going too far and losing ourselves. Perhaps we're in here because it's a wrong diagnosis, or maybe you were just in here because we need the extra love that our families and friends weren't able to provide for us. They didn't have the time or didn't know that you needed it because you're so stubborn. You pretend to be so strong. Whatever the cause, we all ended up here, and we're all stuck under the same rules and regulations contract signed 72-hour hold that usually gets extended to a minimum 1-month stay, the whole thing it really does make you feel like a number.

Trays are down on the table already as we sit and await our morning's fate. You see, the other patients cower over the countertop. This one girl is still lying down on the sofa tall and thin, one of the smallest BMI's I've ever seen with the naked eye. She's asked to join us by Bary, our meal nurse, Bary sits at the head of the table he's also the one who places our trays on the table before we get there, looks at them, inspects them, and he's always there to check plates for missing components. Say if the kitchen accidentally sent up a tray with missing milk, it would be there before we even knew it was missing. Bary, he means well, and he's got some excellent stale humor. That's why I think he's still the meal nurse.

Since meals are the worst time of the day for the disordered eating patients, shit goes down. I mean like tantrums, kids flinging food, trays, anything they could get their hands on like their 2-year olds. Sometimes it gets bad enough where the nurses call in security and the head RN to come in a sedate whoever decides to have a complete meltdown. We take our seats and Lara, the tall thin girl on the couch, finally, moseys on over and takes her spot at the table. Which, by chance, is located right next to my tray. Bary gets all of our attention and starts the clock. I'm fearful because I know we only have 30 minutes. If we don't finish in time, we get the ensures. I lift up my trays lid an am disgusted. They haven't changed the menu the same old nasty eggs and bacon. Slimy surgery maple syrup crystals and makes me think that it will just build up on the walls of my insides forever staying there and ever making me fat. That's all I get on my plate for now. Winter, the nutritionist, will, of course, increase my meal plan by which her equation will, in the end, make me "healthy." She doesn't tell you that she plans to have you leave the program on the larger scale of your healthy zone, calling it "insurance weight" because they pre predict our relapse. Wow, thanks for having faith. I'm not talking about an

extra snack. I'm talking about finding ways to pack down from
5,000 to 10,000 calories a day. So, Lara is sitting next to me
staring, and everyone else is staring at their own tray me being
the observant one is looking at everyone else and am fascinated.

I immediately feel a smirk growing more substantial on my face
when I see Lara take her plastic silver wear package and take the
knife out and hold onto it like it's a toy a small child finally has
to give up but doesn't want to. Hell, I thought she's probably just
going to make love to her wrists or inner thighs later who needs
boyfriends when you have sharp objects, but to my surprise, she
doesn't try and hide the knife she just keeps poking around at
her food then *bam* noise from around the hall distracts Bary.
He turns his front body to see the commotion. Right then, Lara
opens the lid of her peanut butter and dives the knife headfirst.
She takes the edge, plunging it around all the corners, scrapping
every bit. Lara strategically lifts her paper placemat sitting
between the food and the tray, smears all of it against the bottom
of the paper, and squishes it back onto the tray. That's it done,
Lara 1 nurses 0. Let's say this type of behavior is encouraged in a

sickly way, between the patients, and the skill level is based on experience and intelligence, welcome to the real hunger games.

After eating, however long that might take you, you have to get the nurse's attention. He or she will check you off as a pass, or you have to scrape your plate, and if you don't finish in time, you all know supplements. After being checked off, you have to sit in a line of sight (LOS) for an hour, everyone stirs to the Dayroom, and no one is allowed in their rooms. I find a semi, comfortable place to lay down. A sunny spot on the ground, I bend down, nearly falling over. Curled up feeling gross, bloated, fat, I want to disappear. I'm not allowed. The next group is about to start. No one jumps up to go, but one by one, undoubtedly, we all trickle into the movie room that has a makeshift group circle made out of the waiting room office chairs the so pathetically call furniture.

PROCESS GROUP

We're all in for 10 am group therapy. We're all just staring at each other; no one is talking Sussy disclosed the group before proceeding with acknowledging others' needs, which she needed to, it's policy. People are so prone to sue it's crazy. With the type of families that come through here, I can only imagine what people have tried previously. The room is still quiet, silence, nothing. Then one of our councilors works to break the ice by asking questions. One-shot, two-shot, three. Nothing, not one response. All of a sudden, this girl named Alex, who was about to graduate, started to talk about her feelings and emotions, and then there you go once one person starts telling everybody has something to say. I watch the whole time frantically shaking my legs as did Lara, who knows maybe I can learn a thing or two before I get out of here. Group ended.

We all headed out to the day room again this time to be called back into the kitchen for a snack. I was fuming, I was currently used to eating nothing, not a single serving of anything for weeks, and they expect this already? Let's say I tried to convince them my body was not physically capable of holding any more substance, but the nurse didn't have it at all. I was supposed to have something tangible like a piece of fruit or bar, but I couldn't handle it. The nurse brought me a 4oz apple juice and said I had 15 minutes to drink it, or it was going to be an ensure. Some of these rules I don't understand! How is that a fair exchange!? I tried to drink it this time with trembling hands and took baby sips, but my whole body started shaking. I couldn't control anything. I felt pain. The most pain I have felt in a long time, I was hyperventilating and shaking. I let my head fall in between my legs and tried to gasp for air. I was having a panic attack, and my whole body started giving out. I guess I was making a disturbance because the nurses tried to help me to my room; they ended up having to drag me all the way there because both my legs gave out, and I couldn't move them at all. Arms over a nurse on each side of me, I was taken away to my bedroom. They laid me down to my bed, and I immediately turned to the floor and threw up everywhere, everything I had since the minute I left that dining room table my first night admitted. After that, I passed out and thanked God I had finally felt tired enough to do so. Come blackness I've been waiting for you for a while.

I awoke only to step outside the door and realize that I slept hours, and it was around late afternoon. I walked out to the day room to find the group sitting in another circle talking about their issues. I sat and observed. Not ready to speak. I got a couple of pats on the back for making it back out into the Dayroom today. Great. I'm just happy I skipped lunch, but just like clockwork, its snack time again. Since I'm up and out of my room, I have to participate. You're kidding me. Okay, well, here goes nothing. I tried to get out of it by throwing a fit and accusing them of overfeeding me because of what happened this morning, but not going to lie part of me was so hungry that I wanted to eat again. So, I ended up participating. I must have been starving from vomiting earlier. I can also hear the voice. "Fatten up as soon as you can lazy fuck and get the hell out of here" is all I can hear her say. "Get "recovered" as you call it."

Dinner is not too far around the corner. Food is never too far around the corner in 3 East B. Sometimes, I wonder if they don't understand that it's not about the food it's about the way you feel emotions how you handle situations; you know you're fright or flight. If they didn't focus so much on the food, we would get more breakthroughs and fewer relapses. From my personal experience, adolescents in inpatient hospitals, most of them don't eat anything. They get out because of their uncooperative nature. Then their insurance runs out. They get the feeding tube and bragging rights until they become a liability. Or they eat everything, then lose all the weight as soon as they get out of hospital they relapse hard-core (i.e., my plan). They're all recipes for disaster.

SUPPER

You can always smell the scent of dinner cooking through the vents of the hospital wafting in poising your nostrils with the toxic grease, fat, and salt every chef drenches with their dishes. You don't have to guess what the next meal is anyhow because of the meal chart. Remember the one they tape to the wall I was staring at earlier. A laminate meal chart for the whole week taped up on the window next to the makeshift tables they set up on the unit.

As I mentioned earlier, Saturday's dinner consisted of a buffet-style dinner served by the LVNs who watch us. We're allowed to monitor what they dish out on our plates, but we cannot interfere with how much or how little they put on it. They have 1/4 cup portion spoons to measure out the food, or else we would all be getting more significant portions. The buffet displayed upon the kitchen island provoked me. I could almost hear the paper plates mocking me. I let out a big sigh and begun to get in line. Hands shaking, I grabbed my plate. The eating disorder backed me up, calming me down, telling me that everything will be alright when I get out. Everything will be back as the way it was. So I showed up with a smile, made sure the line of the 1/4 spoon where the food was supposed to stop, and went on with my dinner secretly feeling like shit. After dinner, we had free time, and I spent the remaining time puzzling by the window where Roldly and Samm came to sit by me. We leisurely tried to put it together to pass the time. I think of how many hands have been on this thing. I stop putting it together.

Just then, Samm starts asking questions about me, about Rodly and that's when the friendship began. She probed us on everything from where we lived to what our favorite bands were at the time. I absorbed her. She was so enticing. Samm is about 14 and already stunning for her age. She has a square face with sunlight blonde hair that naturally curls as if her hair has been kissed by ocean waves, a smile that could light up a room and grit with a little wit that makes her on top of her game. I learned she has been in residential and just transferred here. She tells us tales of residential. She doesn't speak of her family. She finishes telling us her story, and I realize she hasn't had a Christmas home in three years. I immediately feel empathy for her. I have an impulse to hug her, but I don't.

Roldly is tall Latin bronze skin and dark hair, his skin was paler than average, and you could noticeably tell. He was thin for his tall structure, and even though he was a boy, part of me envied his advantage to get skinner as a boy. He told us he is from the bay area, and this is not his first relapse either. Lost in thought, I wonder how hard it is for women to lose weight and keep it off compared to men because of the biology of it all. I sigh to myself once again, distracted by my thoughts. Samm, Rodly, and I talked the evening away. We discussed personal weights, rituals, and gossiped about the staff. Time was turning on the clock and flew by a lot faster than it usually did. Since none of us had family or friends coming, we ended up talking in that spot during visiting hour up until evening snack.

I grabbed 1Tbs peanut butter and ritz crackers. I didn't care who was around me. It was what was available. I justified my choice, but I secretly craved it. I enjoyed every bite of that snack combination. At home, I would starve for days at a time, my longest streak being 14 days without any solids and only labeled zero calorie liquids. I remember the day I decided to break the fast, never really had fasted like that before. I was with my mother and sister at the pizza place. I didn't eat pizza because I was dieting, and it's forbidden in the dieting world. I agreed to go meet up with my sister and her friend at Round Table.

I wasn't hungry at all. I thought I could go and get a diet soda. I tried to encouraged myself to have some social time. I didn't know how weak my willpower was that day. My mother and I walked in and met my older sister and her friend, who went for the buffet lunch. I personally hate buffets. People can never control their portions. I could never control my portions. We sat with them for a while we all caught up and chatted, the smells in the restaurant started to get stronger, and the hunger in the pit of my stomach roared louder not letting me ignore the loud ED voice in the back of my head.

I can only shut the voice up with the pounding of running legs against the pavement. I looked around at all the food as my mouth salivated and my sister asked me if I wanted to grab something from the pizza bar, I thought what the hell I've been good. I'll peek over there. I took her plate and slowly started towards the foot of the food bar. The smells were dancing around me, singing sweet songs, making me crave them. I felt like a man lusting over a woman how obsessed I was with food. I spotted the breadsticks, my weakness, but there were cinnamon brown sugar ones. Okay, just a few of those sweet little gooey delights will be alright, next thing I in a state of reverie going over for more and more until the people who worked there told me I'd had enough. It didn't stop there I went home and devoured peanut butter by the heaping spoon smearing it all over Ritz crackers and pretzels. I couldn't stop. Just mindless in front of the TV only thinking about the food and I bloated up like a balloon I looked pregnant, but I was still not full, I ate until I got sick I never got the feeling of being full anymore. I Have ignored the hunger pain signals for too long to notice them. So I never know when I'm starved or stuffed. I eat until I'm in a food coma. The next morning the voice is reminding me it's there "Bloated, irresponsible, waste of space. The gross habitual traits you have developed is beyond me. I can't describe how disappointed and disgusted I am at the thought of you. You wanted to trust me, but you can't fight yourself enough to stay on track for even just a day. Your pathetic."

I replay this vivid memory in my head over and over. The memory won't shut off. As we wait for night meds, I think back to where I went wrong.

The lies I told myself took me down the rabbit hole, where I feel safe in slowing killing myself. Where the weight of the world causes me to think too much and eat too little. The lies I told myself and still tell myself lead me to be afraid. The lies gave me a false sense of control, and now I'm trying to get rid of the lies in treatment. I remember just feeling so ashamed of myself I didn't leave the house for three consecutive days after that. I didn't eat for three days after that either. I needed to punish myself. That was my first binge a long time ago, but peanut butter and Ritz are still one of my favorite binge foods. I was quietly reveling my mini binges at snack time in inpatient and justified that "I HAD" to put on weight not to feel guilty about it. No luck. I felt guilty every time I put something through my mouth anyway.

MEDS

Andii, the med nurse, wheeled in with the night medication.
Patients swarmed over to him like bees looking for sweet nectar.
Pop 1, pop 2, pop 3, I am watching all the patients get their
sleeping medication expecting another sleepless night for myself.
Hopeless, I walked away only to be interrupted and called back
by the med nurse. I turned to the cart, took the little paper cup
form Andii, and stared at the little white pill sitting at the
bottom, shifting around as I moved the cup. Ambien, let's dance
lady. Take me through the night with ease. I've been waiting.
After I drowned the little white circular helper, we rounded up
for the night group at 9 o'clock.

All the level 1 unit patients are summoned to their empty cold
bedrooms, which includes me because I just got here. I'm not
even on level one. We're all graced with level zero upon arrival,
but I'll make my way up the level system slowly. I'll manipulate

each care worker and each nurse to get to the top and out of here like I did the last time. I wonder how long my parents are going to be paying off these bills, and my thoughts are once again interrupted by group starting. During the night group, we all go around and rate the day on a scale of 1 to 10. You say how you're feeling. We also don't have to give any feedback at this time, and I never knew why. Indefinitely we all go around and listen to exciting excuses for why each person is unhappy as shit and depressed. I listen to the others in the circle. Some patients don't say anything at all and pass completely, then we go off and listen to the nurse jab on about who gets to stay up. We listen to her talk about what levels, what times bedtimes are, and sometimes it's as if were treated like we're in kindergarten. Not going to lie, some of the patients here need to get treated that way. Maybe they were never treated strictly, and their inner child is longing for structure.

I found it demeaning. We also get requests at this time, so we get to ask the nurse to ask our doctor or write a letter to get answers to our complaints quicker. If you wanted some medication, you didn't have to wait to see your doctor. That was the only part about night group patients at 3 East B seemed to like. Everyone asked for loads of medication than usual to keep the mundane life here at the ward complaisant. It's more accessible to comatose. Going into my bedroom 45 minutes after I had tilted my head back and swallowed that little itty bitty pill that sat at the bottom of my cup earlier, I started to feel drunk. I felt wasted without becoming nauseous.

I guess I was loud or giggly with Samm because all I remember was giggling a lot and then sent to bed. When I got to the bedroom, I danced a bit around. I felt loose for the first time in a long time. I know I wasn't of age to drink, but we all did it anyway. We drank, smoked, popped pills. It was not out of the norm for my small town. When I got my eating disorder, I stopped drinking. I wouldn't allow myself to intoxicate with the caloric value of such drinks that let you feel like you're out of control. My aversion changed later, leaving me to become an alcoholic, but I'm getting ahead of myself. I fell asleep only to be told the next morning by my roommate that I was overly loud, doing a lot of mirror checks in the window. I couldn't remember a thing. Officially my first blackout and it was prescribed to me.

That vacantly opened my eyes to the furor on prescription drugs and how I had an understatement and better perspective of the lost souls in the prescription world. I knew it was lousy, something that shouldn't have gotten me excited, just another bandaid. Another escape from reality. Then you abuse it. Your life becomes a mess of wasted space, and you end up in Betty Ford, but I am far too ahead of myself again. I will talk about my drug and substance abuse treatments on a later date, in another book. For now, back to the eating disorder world.

ITINERARY

As I get more in the routine of being in the inpatient ward, yet again, the motions feel natural. I survey the breakfast trays to see what noxious add ons our meals get so each ED patient can reach the 5,000 to 10,000 daily calorie intake. The pain we go through. In between meals, most of the patients that have eating disorders curl up in a ball in the sun or nap on the couch. Let me try and explain what we go through.

Let's start with what life in a day looks for me at the moment, with some added commentary: Vitals, meds, breakfast, group, snack, feel like you're going to lose control, eat, bear the pain. As bad as every mealtime is for us sometimes, they have their highlights. That usually depends on which counselor is with us and trust me; they had some characters working in the clinic. Personally, I liked having this one guy named Bary sit with us. He would start games with us. Distract the new and scared Ed patients. He knew how to make the stubborn crack a smirk.

Observant in his own and willing to steer off the setlist of maniac rules that come with this place if he thought the rules were too hard on us. He was compassionate and stern, reasonable, and respectful. He would let us slide a little bit.

Sometimes during the week, you would have to see your team and create more plans of action on your case. The doctor only saw one patient a day. So if you were lucky to have an appointment, you would be called out of the group to have an individual session. The rest of the day looked like this: Free time, yoga, or another physical activity if you were privileged enough to move a limb. That's level 2, and as I stated previously, you start at 0. The level system here is a bit obtuse. From what I've observed, if you participate, make it to the end of level 3, your good. Then they think about your discharge and your progress the entire time you been an inpatient. It doesn't take them long after making it to level three before they let you go. Have they even tried hard enough to make sure we are going back to a stable environment? In my experience and observation in EDIOP, inpatient, and Partial Hospitalization Patient (PHP) no, they don't. The team tries to help. The social worker tries to help you find the right location to go back to if you have that choice. The therapist attempts to provide you with coping mechanisms. The doctor solicits prescriptions to you so your head can find a balance.

If you are uncompliant, your team can only do so much for you until they have no choice but to let you go. Now back to the schedule. Dinner is next, then free time or visiting hours. Friends or family cared enough or had the opportunity to come to see you. You had a chance to see them. My mom was lucky enough to get her boss to collaborate with her. So she could drive a few hours to see her non-intentional suicidal daughter that was locked away. I'm stubborn, but my eating disorder is inauspicious. She would lash out anyone who got in the way of our relationship, even if it made me feel guilty after. Anorexia, the one who leers around my shoulder every time I pace the aisle in the grocery store, every time I pierce food with a fork, spoon, or knife. The only thing that keeps the blood pumping in my veins every time I look in the mirror and only see what she wants me to see. Blinding my reality into hers and not even unconditional love can save me. If you're lucky enough for someone to protect you from insanity, you only have an hour.

Visiting hours are from 6 pm to 7 pm. Then the privilege of hearing others live their lives sends you into memories of a time when you had a life of your own even if it was your life was simple. Time elapses, the visiting hour is up. The only non-routine you get besides conversation during a visiting hour is outings around the block from the hospital. To go to the drug or liquor store and peek at new items on the shelf. I swear the world moves fast, and if you eliminate yourself from facing your fears, in reality, you stop progressing. Society keeps going only to put you further back from your goals and aspirations.

You got yourself here, behind sealed doors, and who knows, maybe you'll find yourself here because before you were lost. Perhaps with all this idle time, you can find the courage to face those fears that lead you to the psychiatric ward. It is better than at home. It is better than the reality you created yourself from the years of living in the external world. I didn't know what lifestyle I liked better yet. Maybe that's why I always found myself returning to rehab. I couldn't decide if I wanted a different lifestyle than the comfortable routine I was in that was killing me. The last thing on the list next to meds and round up is night snack. Night snack is our last consuming period for the day. Opting out isn't an option. You get handed the snack they give you. Unless you're on a higher level, you can barter your snack for something equivalent to the nutritionist exchange list. I'm just handed and forced to eat what the nurse gives me because Winter is taking her sweet time setting up our appointment. I always provide the nurses with an easy time about what snack they give me because I know if I talk up, there's a chance they'll shove an ensure on the table and force me to ingurgitate it.

Snack looked different for everyone. Eating disordered patients can feel like meals are lasting forever or seconds, depending on how your ED whispers in your ear, guiding your thoughts. I've seen patients wolf down entire meals in 5 minutes, only to be told to slow down because of their choking. Some patients stare at the food like it's a gift from the Cheshire Cat that will expand your limbs until you're twice the size you once were. I always find myself—staring, observing, and lost in thought—battling with the never-ending screaming that comes from the demons within me. There are only five more minutes of the permissible time. I have to force myself to consume down whatever I procrastinated to eat. Finally, we all walk falteringly to our rooms.

GETTING TIRED OF IT

Nights are always the loneliest times. Around 9 pm, non-levelers slowly drag their remaining mental energy to their rooms at this time, which includes me. I stare at the linen on the bed. White, pure, I look around the room silence enhanced with shuffling noises coming from the hall. I peek through the window on my bedroom door. It is there to allow the nurses to do night checks, but half the time, they waltz right in and shine their blazing LED flashlight in the room and on your face disturbing your dormancy. They are always on the lookout for exercisers, self-harmers, patients with compulsive thought processes that make them act out. I step inside the bathroom that is conveniently in my room.

We're not allowed any makeup, so there's nothing to clean off today. I try and examine myself in the small 4x7 metal plate bolted onto the wall. It drives me mad that I can't see anything. Irritated I walk out of the bathroom and open the blinds, the window at night is the perfect substitute for an actual mirror, and I can see my whole body. I start by caressing my collar bones, neck, face, stomach from both sides, thighs, thigh gap, and eventually, everything else. I don't have Ambien tonight. The order for it was misplaced. Or at least that's what the nurse told me. I got melatonin instead.

I'm wide awake. I walk over to the bathroom again, mentally timing out the nurse's night checks so I can be in bed when she walks in. Inside the bathroom, I settle on the floor and start exercising. I'm doing sit-ups, leg lifts, and the rest of my routine with tears streaming down my face because it's not good enough, I'm stuck here. My anxiety is climbing. The tiles are pushing against my body to remind me of how weak and lazy I've been. My bones and body don't hurt as much lying on the hard ground. I can no longer feel each protruding vertebrae violently hit the hard surface. If it doesn't hurt, it's not good enough because beauty is a pain, and if you're not in pain, you're not beautiful. Trying to neglect my thoughts, I pick up the speed. Going as fast as possible, I raise awareness that the nurse is about to pop her head in, so I push myself up and climb into bed, clammy from anticipation. Instead of continuing my workout, I stay in bed afraid of getting caught. My mind starts racing. Everything that makes me continuously frustrated comes flooding to my forefront. I try and hold back tears, but there's no hope, I weep. Tired from crying, I fall asleep right after the nurse comes in and walks out.

The next time I open my eyes, daylight is creeping through the blinds. I lay in the fetal position and already start to feel perspiration form on my forehead and under my arms. The anxiety of not knowing my weight is itching at me. In my experience, my body magically gains a large sum of density or drops to oblivion. I've never experienced it leveling out. The numbers go up or down. They never stay the same. I'm lying there assuming I've already gained weight from yesterday. The thought kills me. It makes me angry and non-responsive. I want to recluse from the day from the world, but I know if I do that, I'll never get out of here, so I plaster on one of my daily fake smiles and head out the door to retrieve my bathroom supplies and get my vitals done. I walk out to the front room and find myself alone. I guess everyone's at a late start. I go to the nurse's station and check out my items. I head to the nurse to take my vitals then weight. In an eating disorder clinic, you never get to know your weight because they blindly weigh you, which means they weigh you backward. However, there are a few points of measurement that you can account for yourself. For example, when they take our blood pressure, they pull out all the sizes of cuffs. God forbid if they sling the adult size around your arm.

Eyes tightly shut as I feel the nurse wrap the woven synthetic material around my arm I feel her press the Velcro down firmly almost as if it was going to leave a bruise. The pain from her touch elevated the feeling of anxiety enough for me to open my eyes. Not enough for me to care about the extreme pressure of her gesture because my mind is preoccupied with the cuff sizes. I look down and see white. I'm safe. The children's cuffs are white; the adult ones are blue. I grab the box with my name labeled on it containing my showering products and tread back to my room a little more at ease, knowing my cuff size. I guess that's what happens if you can't measure your body in weight? You tend to come up with more creative ways of measuring yourself. Once in the shower, the ease of knowing my cuff size that faded my anxiety melts away because I'm immediately distracted by the size of my lower abdomen.

I know I'm retaining water. It crosses my mind that I have to see the dietitian and tell her about some of my "allergies," also known as masked fears of eating certain unsafe foods that I will not or have not allowed my body to have. Therefore, I am now allergic to them like my lactose intolerance because of my vegan diet. I silently thank the biological standpoint of adaptation for that. I let the nurses know about my diet, and they'll give me exchanges until I can meet with Winter (the dietitian). After taking a shower and putting on a considerable amount of oversized clothing, I make my way out to the day room where the smells breakfast poison my senses. The tray stand is waiting by our table; some of the patients are sitting on the couches. Some are not out of their rooms yet. I take my place at the table with my raw emotions after inhaling the scent of breakfast. I try and tolerate the feelings that come with recovery. My recovery depends on a lot of things. It depends on how willingly I'm ready to let my compulsive urges go. It depends on me for survival.

I guide my attention back to the breakfast trays. I walk over and start to go through them to find my dish. As I do this, I notice another eating disorder patient approach me. I can feel an introduction coming on. She starts by saying hello. Not wanting to chat but anything to distract me from what we're about to consume, I retort. "Hey."

We exchanged the automatic size-up and comparisons anyone with body dysmorphic disorder has and started talking. We talked about our past, where we were from, how long we've been this way, the typical small talk conversation that you have when your labeled eating disorder. She never gives out her name. I leave it alone. Our conversation turns to the trays. We greedily check all the plates to compare ours to the other patients. I'm starting to feel more anxious as I find more calories to count on my tray but also relieved that mine is the lowest amount for breakfast. Easing into my chair at the table, I start talking with Samm, the blonde from the puzzles. She must be about 3 or 4 years younger than me, but with this disease, you never know I mean a 30-year-old can look like she or he is 18, and if you have had this disease long enough, it will prematurely age you. Samm and I are starting to become more comfortable with each other. It's incredible how many similar interests we have. I learned she had Anorexia for half of her life already. She only had a few short years of carelessness. To be drawn into this horrible disease at an age so young is heartbreaking. I've won the lottery being able to live out my youth and not have the illnesses that rule my mind taint my childhood. Samm's been in treatment for a while now. So have I. Hopefully, this time, we can get through recovery together.

The gossip comes to a full stop when the trays are slammed down on the table in front of us, causing silence. Also, by this time, all the ED clients are at the table. Ours is the largest table in the kitchen just in case another outlander gets imprisoned, I'm assuming. Fascinated with the other patient's trays, I leave the plastic lid on top of mine. I start picking at the safe foods provided next to the cover of the tray. I begin with the grapes. I watch others. See if I can pick up any more tricks. Popping the grapes into my mouth seems so foreign. I look up to see the table struggling just as hard as I do feel a bit better about my hesitation and struggling compliance. The sweet and salty smells dancing around my nose makes my stomach growl, and my body begs for the meal placed before it. How could my body still want food if I look pregnant, stomach distended to the size of a small ball, growing every day because of the amounts of food we have to eat. I'm trying to convince myself that it is only temporary. It's a constant battle between the mind and the body. Fifteen minutes pass by, and I've finished the grapes. I struggle to start the main meal.

THE HABITS WE SHARE

What will cause a person to do unmentionable things without really thinking about it or controlling their actions? Anxiety.The other non-eating disordered patients get it sometimes if they've ever had a near-death experience if they've ever truly meant to kill themselves. They get it. I have major anxiety over this meal right now. My thoughts are a perfect distraction for not eating, and time is about over. I kick myself and pick up my fork. While I am picking at my main course, I look over at Lara. She is staring at the nurse sitting with us, and the nurse is reading, so she's a little distracted. Lara swiftly takes her pat of butter, drops it in her lap, folds it into a napkin, and the napkin vanishes. I think I'll sit next to her more often. I take off the lid I have been hesitant to lift. Yellow scrambled eggs that jiggle in a certain way to make you think they are reheated. Two sausages that were most likely frozen before cooked and covered in grease. Seeping, oozing, fatty grease making me sick just looking at it. Glory, the nurse, starts yelling at a Hana to stop cutting up her pieces small. Lara takes her cream cheese and spreads just enough to know she used it on the corner of the bagel she has to eat. I take a mental note. Meanwhile, Alex finishes and has Glory come check her tray off so she can excuse herself from the table. Glory walks over to her feet heavy on the ground. Shaking the tables with each footstep. As soon as Glory makes her way over to Alex, Lara takes the rest of her cream cheese in her right hand. While Glory's facing away, Lara scrapes the cream cheese into the napkin on her lap. She then shoves the packaging back onto her tray. Making it look like the cream cheese was eaten. I start to gander at all the remaining items that take up wasted space on my tray and eliminate the contents figuratively. Then literally, I start to eliminate items by the methods I can use. My soy milk, I can ditch that at the end of the time slot because you can pierce the top with the straw (you have and pretend to sip on it occasionally throughout eating the rest of your meal) at the end when the nurse checks your tray all you have to do is turn the carton upside down. Depending on how you pierce the carton, you can prevent it from spilling out when you do the whole 180, amazing, right? So, there's an item to check off the list. It becomes the hunger games; everything is more fun when you make a game out of it. It's too easy in here to do so. I slowly finish what's on my plate and ask to be excused. The nurse checks my tray. I hold my breath as I tilt the soy milk carton upside down, not even a drop spilled I'm good to go. Feeling good about not having to drink my soy milk, I secretly congratulated myself. I allowed myself to curl up in the sun as a reward, because of line of sight retreating to my bedroom would not be an option until later. At home, my comfortability of being around others after a meal was non-existent. I can't eat in front of other people. Right after eating, if going to my bedroom was unachievable, I would or go on a walk by myself. Just to avoid all the noise. I freak out if people talk about food or ask questions about what I'm eating, always. At EDIOP, I had to sit with a pillow on my lap right after eating with the group because I couldn't stand the thought of my stomach having food in it, it couldn't digest anything, or it felt as if it couldn't. I know that the secretion in my organs made the digestion process slower because food had become a foreign object to my body, and it didn't know what to do with it. So the food sat, like a large parasite that infected my internal organs. It sat there, making me feel sluggish and pathetic, mocking me any chance my wandering mind had space; it was filled with nasty remarks to myself, reminding me I'll never be good enough. I stayed in the sun long enough to fall asleep. A quick cat nap curled up on the floor in the Dayroom. Peaceful and relaxed, my moment of serenity was interrupted by the calling of a process group, where we all pretend to be happy or make it as dramatic as possible to get the most attention. One by one, we weave to the chairs formed in a perfect circle created by Sussy, the most irritating counselor by nature. She's pretty and kind and always dressed accordingly like nothing in the world bothers her. Maybe it doesn't, but I'm sure that she masks some of her urges to release the beast upon us because of the fear of letting her guard down. To be called a bad representation, we all have those egos, don't we? Anyway, we're all sitting in the circle now, squirming to find a comfortable position. I get yelled at for fidgeting and wanted to burn extra calories. I shake it off with compassionate looks from the other patients who also get yelled at for constantly standing and moving around. Hana, one of the ED patients, would walk around the entire kitchen and Dayroom all the time. I was curious, so I asked her what she was doing, she traced the top of one of the tables that looked like one of the tables you would find in your elementary school cafeteria. She made it to the end of the table, tracing it delicately as if she was conserving her time to answer the question. Finally, she said it was to burn more energy. She couldn't stand the thought of being stuck in here and being forced to sit and do nothing. Confined to one large room and an outside patio that we only get to go out on for about an hour a day. It's the only thing that keeps her sane. While I mentally check off another trick for the books, I remind myself to write down habitual routines I observe mainly for researching the obscurity of this disease, to test the limits. If anyone had the willpower and curiosity to explore new avenues of this disease, it would be me.

PLANS

2 pm Winter walks into the day room. The eating disorder patients swarm around her like she's a God. Here that title might fit her job. She controls every morsel that goes in our bodies, every grain of salt. Every distinctive need and request doesn't begin unless she approves. Winter, our nutritionist, our frienemy. I need to make my move to talk to her. I can't keep eating this crap they give me, so I start thinking about all the dietary needs I can get away with before I approach her. I start visualizing a mental list to break open these ideas to her softly. I'll start by addressing her needs, so she thinks she's in control, and I'll get straight to the points I want to make after. I will hear her out because she knows me. She knows I've relapsed under Alta Bates hospital care, and I need to know what she has planned for me. As I'm brainstorming, my thoughts are rudely interrupted by the sense of a lingering presence. You know that

feeling you get when someone is hovering over your shoulder or that urge you have to look around because you can feel eyes press hardly on you. I got one of those feelings only to look up and see Winter's mouth stretched ear to ear, smiling at me. Her smile quickly fades into sympathy. She frowns a little probably to let me know that she's sorry I have returned just then she says what I'm thinking.

"Sorry to see you back here, Hun," her frown deepened.

"Yea, I'm sorry too," was all that I could muster.

"So let's just get straight to business" she starts to pull out the food chart so I can pick away at the mental list I was preparing earlier.

"Can you please mark off your allergies, and we'll work around them" ten seconds later, done...she continues.

"I would also like you to start intaking as much as your last release day because your stomach settled down a bit, and we know you can handle it physically (AKA we know you don't have refeeding syndrome). We also need you at a higher weight than you were when you first left because of your relapse."

Great I thought, that already makes me distrust her. You can't trust her, said the voice in my head.

"Um ok, I just want to get out of here" was my final reply, not fake enough anymore to plaster on a smile and say everything's ok after our quick interaction. My team knows I've relapsed, and they think I'm playing a game. For me, it's a game, but it's also not a game; it's a perfectly imperfect coping mechanism. It works for me. I don't feel the pressures of anxiety and stress while restricting and exercising. It was learning how to love myself then basically morphed into a 101 on how to learn to hate myself.

INCREASED PORTIONS

Time was pressuring into the afternoon. Snack was approaching
again. It seems as if a snack or a meal is always around the
corner. Ritz with peanut butter was my snack, and I rolled my
eyes and sighed. At first, I was having my usual snack without
guilt because I had less for my meals. Now I clandestinely
panicked about it. Handling the voice in my head was the hardest
to cope with; it continually makes me feel horrible. I feel guilty
and hate myself more if I don't give it any of my attention. I took
the opportunity to distract myself by frantically thinking of ways
to dispose of even the smallest amount of my snack. That is how
I kill time waiting for the other patients to take their seats at the
table. It was a game we all liked to play, so when we began
eating, I took a cracker in one hand and the Tbs of peanut butter
in the other. I sneakily crumbled the bread so the edges would

fall to the floor. I was successful. The peanut butter, however, I couldn't dispose of this time. I did manage to leave some plastered to the side of the tiny container and lid. We have to tilt the used package to the nurses to ensure we have eaten all the scrappings. I maneuvered it in a way she only saw the packaging no peanut butter in sight. Finally, I was permitted to leave the table, I made sure I scooted the crumbs all around the floor, so I could step on them with my shoe collecting all the crumbs as I left.

I sauntered away from the table half feeling accomplished by the actions that I had just thought of with a mere adrenaline rush. However, I was dissatisfied by having to think about the colossal portions I was dealing with now. My plates now were, without doubt, the most substantial meals on the ward compared to the other ED's now that I've seen Winter. It made me furious. I didn't rebel because I thought that being the people pleaser I am, I could go home faster. I should've resisted like Lara; she always tried to rebel. Yeah, she had to be sent to her room a lot, and she wasn't privileged to do a lot of activities, but she was the thinnest there was no arguing in that. I should've copied Lara because I probably would've gotten out faster, more tenuous. The smart anorexics wait until their insurance is up, then they're kicked out, and sometimes they even manage to lose weight on the ward. I didn't realize that until observing the patient's habitual traits. At the end of my stay, I would witness patients getting kicked it out for non-compliance, thinner when they had arrived. My focus was entirely used by trying to people please, gain discharge, and then figuring out a way to get rid of the extra calories, extra weight, additional this, excess that. I've trained myself to need nothing, and everyone should learn to need nothing because we're all to needy.

After a snack and dusting off the remains of the cracker crumbs from my shoe to the carpet, I briefly met with my doctor. At this point, I think he didn't want anything to do with me because this isn't my first time in the ward, and he knows my history. He probably thinks I will relapse again, I do. He seemed genuinely kind and caring for each of us, but when we wouldn't comply, he would opt out for being passive and turn the other shoulder to show his colder side, letting the nurses act cruelly through his orders on paper. He's the puppeteer, and the nurses are his puppets running the ward by his command. I'm here to gain the weight they already have planned for me. I know what mass they want me to leave at — minimum BMI of 18 plus insurance weight. I despise myself at that surrealistic mass, but it'll be the only way I can get out.

I grit my teeth. Smile the fake smile that the ward has seen repetitively. I am now living for the future and visually putting my mindset to what's to come. This whole gaining weight is just temporary. I will be out fast; I keep as my mantra for sanity. I carried a lot of clout coming in here, and if I can do it once you bet I can do it again, and again. After the real quick visit with my doctor, I got down to the Dayroom. I see some sufferers shuffle around the room. Then a man walks in with a sixty's vibe, long white hair with a beard just enough to look scruff but not overdoing it. His button-down shirt, faded along with his chino raw hem looking pants. His clothes virtually all earth tone colors, including his shoes, Birkenstocks. Did he start pulling out enormous containers with thick opaque color...then brushes, art supplies maybe?

Hopefully, I needed some sort of relief from this stale reality. Then the tables were turned into a makeshift project station. Paper was brought out and spread all around the tables, the room was becoming a temporary art classroom right before my eyes, and I started to feel my insides perk up after that dreadful afternoon with people who have no faith in me. I.e., My treatment team. People who made you feel like another name processed through the file folders of the hospital. Art therapy had begun. All the patients huddled around the tables and stared at the councilor.

I look over at Samm. She seems to be in her world in her head. Maybe she didn't need visuals to escape. She sat there the whole time, tapping her legs against the ground, looking down, not saying anything I felt bad for her, but I couldn't do anything. I kept working on my project, which was nothing of the sort when you think about it because I haven't had any training in sketching or painting. That's one of my problems I noticed this time working on myself. Observations that I make about myself. I saw that I wouldn't start a task unless I know I'm good at it, and that sucks because It causes me to be scared, scared that's what I am a fucking dependent waste of breath that can never make up her mind.

Very sensitive, some might say too painful for the world to handle, I know that because my mom says it to me and she knows me the best. We receive instructions to paint a picture of ourselves when I'm finished with the painting. It comes out okay, I think. We turn to show our images to the group and explain them. I did say art "therapy." I don't feel like showing mine, but I think it's probably better for my treatment. To help me get out of this place, so I share. I don't say much, just let the other patient's opinions flood and drown the sounds of anxious thoughts. They all seemed to notice that I drew myself facing backward I don't know if that necessarily means anything, it means nothing to me, but maybe I should look into it. It might be worth killing time to silence the nagging I get from the perfectionist side of myself that wants to take over. Maybe I'm being haunted by someone who lived a past life and was anorexic, and they are forcing me to these harsh rituals by skipping one meal at a time. Maybe I choose this path before even being born. Who knows? By the time I am done daydreaming, everyone has had a go with sharing their art pieces. We're all left to free time until dinner at six pm...great.

CONFESSIONS & TESTS

My doctor shuffles the paper documents around in the tips of his fingers. He glances up here and there to catch my eye for a split second. He should say Nicole I'm disappointed in you for coming back here, but he's doesn't he keeps fiddling with the documents like he's in between his wife in the bedroom. I stare at the papers refusing to catch his attempts at making eye contact with me while tuning him out. I look around the room, nodding and mhm-ing so he can continue. He blabs on and on about my treatment as I pretend to listen, and when he's finished, I try and make a fast one out the door. I'm stopped halfway out the rectangular vortex into the crazy. The doc looks me right in the eyes and says, "Nicole, I'm surprised to see you here again."

I turned and shut the door behind me, a smirk appearing in the form of rebellious actions, and the monster is satisfied. As I enter the Dayroom, the community meeting has already begun. I slide into an empty chair, letting it hold my weight. God knows where it's at now. I'm surprised I don't break the chair. My eyes shut as muffles of the patient's daily feeling on the scale are tossed around to the councilor, Sussy. I let the vibration of other complaints fill the room as I escape into the darkness — my attention perks when my name is called. I chime in my feelings. Indifferent, withdrawn. A couple of minutes pass without me saying much more, just going through the motions.

When the first group ends, we break for five minutes. Feels like seconds when the second group is called. All of us cram into the tv room, which is so tiny it looks like it's fit to be a cubicle. In the middle of the room, a provisional circle awaits us. Empty chairs devoid of people. By the time I enter the room through the narrow doorway, everyone has their place. I sit in the last spot available. The group is introduced as a confidentiality group. We're legally not allowed to say anything out of the group, including the councilors. That is unless they think we're harming ourselves or others. Well shit, I guess we can't say much then, about all of us want to commit self-harm, intentionally, unintentionally.

We sit in solemn silence. I look over at Lara. She's hammering her leg up and down so fast so quickly I can't see the print on her sweats any longer. Ten minutes passed by and were all quiet. This is a joke. Then Lara ups and storms out the door like she doesn't have time for this shit, and I almost follow her out. I hesitate. I don't leave. I remember I'm inside a living board game. You have to follow the rules to pass go. So, we sit in some more silence I decide to talk to get my monopoly piece further to the end of the game. I talk about things that I am unhappy or displeased with to crack the ice. I think the councilors were pleased because we at least talked about something. Time is over before I know it. I'm just happy we got out of the humid room filled with dissatisfied emotions. After lunch, Sussy comes up to me during my free time. She thinks I'm ready for level two, thank God I spoke up during the group she encouraged me to petition tomorrow during the morning group. Collect $200 when you pass GO. Yes, please. The next morning when I requested for a higher level, everyone agreed that I should move up.

Right then, I felt something in my chest, a tingling feeling, possibly a sense of pride. That feeling was almost new to me for how long it had been absent. Relishing the feeling of achievement was powerful. It made me feel as if I was worth something more than my negative thoughts, but pessimistic thoughts stripped that pride. As I glanced up at the clock, there was no more time to get perplexed with positivity — time for the next. Time cannot waste. The next group consisted of "school," which is a pathetic name for another art class. During this time, we are given coloring handouts and are encouraged to journal and draw. There is not a lot of education here, but I guess the RN's aren't teachers.

I've been tugged aside and told I wouldn't be joining "class" today. I watch the group parade out the steal alarm triggered door that's locked from both the inside and outside. I think about what's in store for me this afternoon. I'm pulled into the day room where I find Winter, my nutritionist, and the doc sitting waiting for me to join them. I suspiciously step closer to them, trying to detect any signs in nonverbal communication. Nothing. I take my seat across from them. Winter breaks the reticence by introducing why they have gotten together and requested to meet with me today. She starts by saying I was submissive to the program last time, and the doctor agreed to experiment with me. Then Winter pulled out a machine that was superannuated. She explained that this machine was a body mass index reader (BMR reader). It was to tell me how many calories I burned just sitting down, not doing anything all day. Of course, I want to know how many calories I burn. Admittedly, I didn't think I would burn a lot by breathing and sitting, but the science broke it down to tell me differently. This unpleasant experiment went like this. We gathered in a circle around in the Dayroomday room. Sitting down I put a rubber piece of the apparatus into my mouth it looked like some scuba mouthpiece you breathe out of made for swimming pools, you know the kind that comes with the matching googles you got as a kid. Well, that lovely thing measured the amount of CO_2 in my breath. It measured my inhales and exhales per second. I sat there for 5 minutes. What a dreadfully my long five minutes that turned it to be, and it wasn't pretty.

I drooled the entire time, so not only did I look like a drooling idiot, I looked like a drooling idiot science experiment sitting with my "new colleagues" in awkward silence. Five minutes pass by, covered in pools of saliva, I remove the scuba gear from my mouth. Test results were instantaneous as the machine read back a number higher than expected, 1440 the magical metric number that my body seems to run off of. Shit, it took me by surprise. I just sat there stunned, thinking the machine must have broke. Winter or the doc must have tampered with it to trick me. They finished the conversation and talked about how they wanted to experiment with how much I weigh at discharge. This time they need my target weight higher than it was before. I drop my eyes. That's too much, I'm thinking. "They want to make you fat. Pretend you're okay with it." the voice is back. I can't hold back any longer, and emotions take over, my blood is boiling. I poke and pry with questions of why and how can they do this to me. Hot salty water trails down onto my dry lips the moisture and heat from the tears are the only indication that lets me know I'm crying that I'm upset. One hundred twenty-two pounds is the goal weight they set for me, and I storm out of the room yelling behind me to Winter to just load me up so I can never see them again.

GROUNDHOG DAY

The next morning, I wake up and go through the morning routine with the other ghostly bodies, it's like a morgue in here only the dead are living. We all mosey over to the high table that creates our emotional baggage from day to day and waits for the trays to distribute. My try comes and is full. There is no room left for anything else, not even another pat of butter. Well, I guess Winter heard me when I called out "pile it on" before recoiling back to my temporary sanctuary the other day when we experimented. She honestly piled on the food. I take the longest out of any other patient, but this time I don't take pride in abiding the longest because I know that it's just because there are at least three times the amount on my tray than anyone else. When I finish, I show the head nurse and give myself props for using the breakfast tricks I've been picking up from Lara and applying them where I can. Like I said, It's a game and a competition. You can keep score of the tricks you use until, inevitably, the hospital gets what it wants.

The group starts again. We're all sitting in the tv room. Still, the same as we left it earlier. Stale, humid, emotionless. We begin by repeating our names. We have to do this tedious task at the start of anything we do. I assemble more than just my name this time to show the nurses I'm acquiescing with them. The circle opens up a little bit more. I decide to play therapist rather than the patient as I poke around at others with questions of concern and wonder to distract myself from this limbo. I start to learn more about the other client's backgrounds. I am gaining empathy for them by relating to their experiences. I feel closer to the patients when the group comes to close.

We end the group with some knowledge that there will be free time for the next few hours. I decided to put my level up to use and take the level 2 bin full of coloring supplies back to my room. My Roommate is still level one, so she hopes down on the floor next to me and gazes at the bin with wonder. As I open the top lid, I ask her to join me in my exploration of color and everything that comes with the magic box. Excitedly she agrees and shifts her stance to see inside. With hopefulness to find something undiscovered, she whips out a radio from the bottom of the bin.

"Any preference?" She asks. I shake my head tell her I'm not familiar with the stations. She turns it on. A deadweight lifts from my shoulders as the tunes glide through my ears and sinks into my soul. I've missed music even if it is uncategorized and random coming from a shitty ass radio that blares static once in a while. You think they could invest some of the thousands of dollars our families pay for us to be in the hospital for some better product. Maybe they want us to feel privileged outside the ward. Who cares? I crank up the volume and dance away. My Roommate joins in, dancing with as much energy as possible, trying to burn off breakfast. We finish our free time by drawing then taping our precious art pieces around the room like a modern art gallery. I paste my last inspirational quote on the wall only to wish I was back home so my friends can say it to me.

RN Babe summons all of the eating disordered to the dining room for a snack, we usually pick treats from the cupboard by our exchange rate pass it off by one of the nurses and miserably munch away. However, this morning I am surprised with a unique bar that looks like it could feed a family of four. What's this? Babe responds with a shrug and doctor's orders. He's the worst. They should've never let him work with teens, especially those in need of comfort. He's as cold as ice. Most of us are okay with that because we like a little personality challenge, but he's the type of RN who eats broccoli for lunch in an eating disorder facility, saying it has loads of protein. I mean, come on. A long line of silence fills the room as we each grab our seats at the table. Taboo fills the silence as we each unwrap our non-nutrition labeled snack. They can't trick us. We're all smart enough to know the caloric value of almost everything that's placed in front of us, except for my foreign snack. I tremble as I pick it up. Without hopefulness, I remove the plastic wrap assuming the nutrition was blacked out by Winter's black sharpie. I'm startled as the plastic makes contact with the table upside down, gets stuck, and the nutrition information is in clear view. Without trying to disturb Babe and set off any alarms that I have the calorie content, I slowly turn the plastic wrap, so it's more accessible to read. No that can't be right, I look again only this time I raise the wrapper to my eyelids and draw attention to myself. Noticing other eyes on me, I casually let go of the packaging and watch it drift in slow motion till it hits the floor, and I wish I were dropping down with it. Five hundred calories in this brick of compiled high caloric garbage, I sink lower in my seat. My stomach starts to hurt even before I take my first bite.

I blink my eyes forward to break the stare. If they catch you staring, it might be considered a disordered eating behavior and were trying to win this game. Looking up, my attention is brought back to the room and not just the numb feeling that consumed me when I realized what I told Winter the other day about increasing my caloric intake on the unit was put in motion. Damn, they loaded it up when you asked for it. I don't think loading up a depressed anorexic to the maximum caloric value was a good idea, shit I didn't know what to expect. I was blinded by the thought of returning home and dropping the weight once again. I break a piece of the bar off, allowing as many crumbs as possible to be welcomed by my lap, the floor, the tile — anything but my mouth.

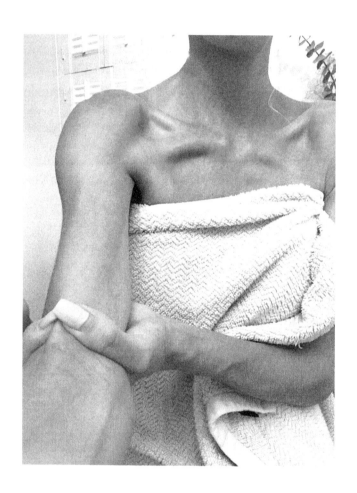

TRUTH, SADNESS, AND GAIN

Bile rises from my throat as a protest against my voluntary actions. My stomach produces too much acid to deteriorate the nutrients that are supposed to keep me alive—leaving me bloated. I ask for an anti-acid and head towards the puzzles in the corner of the room where the window is. Sometimes there are people outside sometimes there's not. A creaking noise interrupts my thoughts as I look up to see Samm and Rodly sit down next to me. Smiles and conversation of mutual hate for this place take up the empty gap as we wait for the next group to start. I can see Nam sitting in the corner of the couch blankly staring outside, probably hoping for a zombie apocalypse to end this common way of survival. He doesn't talk much, but then again, neither do any of us. Nam was born a girl and felt like he should've been a boy. So that's what he is now. He takes testosterone hormones and dresses like a boy, and we all love him the same. Sussy comes in and announces a group. All of us saunter into the tv room to start. No hi, my name is Nicole. I say "Nicole" and turn my head towards the right to set the chain reaction off. The group always begins with the councilors trying to pry us open to speaking. Sometimes they don't make us do anything or talk. We sit in a circle for an hour, going stir crazy. I'm pretending to get better, so the conversation starts with me talking and describing my current situation at home, friends, family pretty much anything to make the time go past. After I speak others chime into what I'm talking about, if they're on a mutual agreement, then it's a whole group conversation with the councilors and everything. I guess it only takes one stream to run into other streams to make a river.....and boy did some patients pour out. I watch puddles form on the tile from a patient's tears because of the session. I ask myself if I instigated anything. I deny the fact and head out the door when it's time to leave.

COMPLIANT

One by one, all of us lurch out to the day room where the tall
man with white hair and a hippie vibe comes to meet us, Jonah
again. Next to him is a tall rack with blocks, straps, Mexican
blankets, and yoga mats. He introduces himself, instructs us to
grab one of each, and then proceed to the floor and find a
comfortable spot in the room. I've never done yoga before. I
don't know if I'll even like it. It's all about being in your body
and being aware of your body and breath. Becoming aware is the
last thing I want to do, but without hesitation, I am docile, grab
everything on the rack, find a spot on the floor, shut my eyes,
and lay down. The faster we can get this over, the faster I can go
back to my room and do nothing and not be in my body. He first
tells us to lie on our backs and be one with our breath and feel
our breath go through our chests to our belly out our lungs. Then
he guides us through some basic stretches. I'm fidgeting the

whole time. I can't stay still. I hate this practice. It's hard for me to enjoy it because it's not a strenuous exercise. I hate the feeling of my body, and in yoga, they always want you to be aware of what's going on with it. I finally give up and just lay there. I feel the tears swell up in the corner of my eyes. It's hard to pretend everything's okay all the time. It's hard to pretend everything will be fine. I just lay there until I see others start to put their equipment away. I roll up my mat, put everything back, and curse yoga under my breath for being so mentally painful. I am not one with my body. I'm in a war with it.

VISITS & FAMILY SUPPER

I usually don't have visitors come during the only hour we're allowed actually to have anyone come. I blame the distance. 6 pm comes around. Those lucky enough to have family close to Berkeley approach and invade the ward. During this time, I usually just put together puzzles in the corner. It passes the time fairly quickly, but to my surprise, I spot my best friend Ashleigh and her boyfriend Kameron out of the corner of my eye. With excitement, I rise from the chair and swiftly walk towards them, embracing the warm human contact I've been craving. At the moment, I'm surprised by myself. I hate touching, hugging, any contact really because of the way I think that they'll judge my now cushioned frame layered with fat now that I'm almost at my ideal weight. We sit and talk about new occurrences in their lives and the mundane ones going on in mine. They ask questions about the ward because who wouldn't want to know what happened a day to day in the loony bin. I share some stories of dull days and exciting ones where patients lose it. Time elapses. I sit back to think how great of friends they are to drive in all that traffic for the tiny visit slot. The only other thing I have to look forward to is our family dinner this week.

Weekly there are family dinners that take place. If your family can't make it or treatment team doesn't think you're ready for this you sit at the usual dining table for eating disordered, but I've passed enough days, enough tally marks on the wall to prove I've been in here long enough to give it a go. Out in the dining room/kitchen is a buffet-style dinner consisted of rice, bbq ribs, corn, juices, bread rolls, salad, and cookies. I have to eat all of it. The usual bare tables are made up of white clothes and centerpieces to make it more formal, to bring a home essence, maybe to dial down the crazy, so we don't scare the sane. It's nothing special the cheaply make the place look like a spaghetti feed, you know the ones where a group of people put on a dinner and show to raise money for a function. The dining halls tables moved to a restaurant-style fashion. Cheap table cloths, floral decorations, and centerpieces are taken out of storage bins and placed on the furniture like a fine restaurant. Families drop in one by one.

My mom arrives last. My stepfather never comes, I'm not his daughter. My sister never comes. She stopped talking to me after my eating disorder consumed my life. My mother and I sit down at one of the tables. My tray, already placed, all the extra food I have to imbibe is on it. I have to go to the buffet and have the LVN's dish out my servings. With my mother, I walk over to the buffet. To my mother's surprise, the LVN's serve her plate too. I can see her eyes grow wide. She doesn't say anything as she watches in silence. We head back to the table and start eating and talking. She tells me about the family, what's going on at home, and her work as she picks her plate. I'm listening and shoveling food in my mouth, trying to keep up with my time limit. She eats the meat on her plate, shuffling her fork around everything else. I think to myself well, at least she's getting protein. At this time, I'm able to sneak the dressing and pats of butter up my sleeve. The LVN's and nurses back off and don't interfere as much during our family dinners. We'll be under the watchful eye of our parents. Or, in my case, my mom.

I know if she catches me hiding food, she won't cause a scene. My biggest worry is not having the LVN's find me doing it as they walk by once every in a while. I manage to get away with all the condiments and slyly smear all the bbq sauce off my ribs and onto the plate, playing it off like gravity did it, not me. I still cut my food into tiny bits and try to get the slivers of meat to blend in with the paper plate. I also leave my milk full and tip it upside down with the straw in knowing that when I show the LVN for clearance, the soy milk won't escape. I don't know how this works, but it does. The cookie on my plate I can't avoid. I crumble as much as I can in my hands, letting the remnants fall to the ground leaving a crumbled mess like I'm a child. We finish and visit for an hour while I talk about how I'm doing in my treatment and how much I want to come home. My mom says she misses me back, and she says she's tried to get me out of treatment, but my doctor said that would be going against medical advice and that the hospital would set out a social worker to come after my her. In reality, I think they want our money and keep us here long enough to watch zeros magically appear by the dozen behind a number on their paychecks, thinking that they have helped us. When mom leaves, I'm a little sad. I calm down a bit, knowing that Ambien will take me away to darkness in a couple of hours.

HEALTHY IN PAIN

Days keep passing. I'm awaken feeling like a stuffed turkey at a Thanksgiving dinner. My meals keep increasing. There is no laxative use allowed. I'm stuck with the feeling of just binged, and the haunting never goes away. My stomach is always full and grotesque. I'm often in pain and uncomfortable. I heard the news from my doctor that I get to go on a pass this weekend, so Gail (my mom) is coming to collect me.

She comes, and I put on a show as always that I'm doing better but, in all truth, it feels good to see her, she has always been my comfort zone, she lets me believe in the impossible and has taught me that the stars are in my grasp. I hate to disappoint her. She's the only one I can turn to when it gets dark in my mind where the shadows cast and demands come out to play. They love to whisper in my ear and send my thoughts into a spiraling vortex of confusion and hate, but I'm getting off track. Stepping out of the ward felt indescribable. I mean, I don't think

I know anyone who has felt that feeling unless you've been locked up against your will and only allowed outside synthetically by access to a patio. We went out to Emeryville. I remember just driving in the car was enough, the breeze on my skin was enough, the smells of different restaurants, the warmth of the sun on my skin, my hair blowing in the wind. Watching other people who are laughing, crying, smiling, all of it was enough. I was starting to see how the program was working. Life around us is beautiful if you see it for the first time again.

As mom parked the car, I finished applying my makeup for the first time in what felt like a century. I almost forgot how annoying it is to put on. I took one last glance in the mirror before opening the door into reality and prepared myself with one last deep inhale and exhale. I knew I had gained weight, and I could feel it everywhere. No hiding it either, but I could hide my feelings, so I put on a façade that nothing was bothering me. We hit every category on girl talk while we shopped. Mom bought me a cute lightweight chambray dress because I'm doing such an excellent job in "recovery" even though I secretly was panicking inside for how much weight I had gained in such a short amount of time. The full-length mirror made Amy eating disorder come out and have a little conversation with me in the dressing room. I felt water welt up on the sides of my eyes from repetitive negative thoughts. I quickly bent forward and watched the tears hit the floor instead of running down my cheeks, leaving no proof of emotion.

I blinked enough times to air out the wet reside in my eyelashes and coated on that same Ol fraudulent smile everyone is so used to they believe it's real. Right before exiting the dressing room, I remember to perk myself up. Then I walk out. I tell my mom I love the dress. A little while later, we leave to have dinner. By this time, I have gotten my phone back from her. Thankful for the distraction of socialism, I do not even realize where we were going. We end up at PF Changs. We were seated right away, greeted by the waitress in a matter of minutes, because of how early we got to the restaurant for a dinner outing. I immediately order a Diet Coke and not a word from mom. She must not care or is just not saying anything, probably the latter. I ordered chicken and rice but then suddenly panic at the thought of the oils and sauces. I make a mental note to be more diligent with my ordering. All the chat catching up with mom during our meal has left me with the upper hand in getting away with shifting my food around the plate. I got away with barely eating anything for dinner. I hope mom didn't notice.

Returning to the clinic was hell. I did not want to go back, but I had an appeal going back because I want to tell my new friends about my outing. It's like having real friends on the outside world and engaging them the gossip over the weekend. I checked into the front office and said goodbye to my mother. A movie was playing. I got my cardigan, wrapped it around me, and plopped down on one of the empty seats in the back row. Samm so happened to be next to me. We started conversing away. I was able to gossip with her by sitting in the back row where no one could hear us. Of course, she asked if I had skipped meals.

I didn't know whether to lie to her or tell her the truth. First of all, I didn't want to trigger her because you don't want to cause anyone to have a setback. Secondly, I feel like when you start restricting or engaging in behaviors and share what you did or didn't do, it becomes an unspoken competition, and I don't want my friend to turn into an enemy. That would be the worst, but Anorexia wanted to boast. There's an unspoken set of rules that you devote your life to when you get drafted into war with this disease. Whenever my Anorexia has a chance to brag, she will. Sometimes they could be the most dangerous instructions, and you would still follow her every word.

We all know she wants death in the end. We all want to be hanging out right on the edge of her game too. We don't wish actually to die. Or at least I didn't, but, in the end, I decided to tell Samm I restricted anyway. Maybe I told her to let her know I was still engaging in behaviors that I was still "pro-anorexia." I don't know. I just wanted her to like me. I thought by telling her I would get points or something that's what happens to your thought process when you have high anxiety. You end up acting stupid or shy or weird because of it. Or you get a competitive eating disorder. I say goodnight to Samm happy knowing that I have become closer to her in that short amount of time. Glad that I am making some good friends.

Walking back to my room, I was thinking about how everyone who shares this disorder is more courteous to me than anyone in my schools were, ever. I opened the door, washed my makeup, watching the black and pink and red drip from my face like a painting that had been sitting out in the sun too long melting away. I changed clothes, lay down on the brick-hard bed waiting for my meds to help me drift off to sleep. As I was lying there, I remembered my meeting with the doctors and my family tomorrow. I cringe a little.

RECOVERY EMOTIONS

Today was not a good day. Not a day to highlight on the calendar.
Last week I had a great outing (well made it seem significant for
all the eyes around me, I'm a pretty good actress), I've been
steadily going towards my goal with almost zero complaints and
following well, most of the rules. HELLO, doctors, can't you see a
girl trying? Let me tell you how the mind of someone with body
dysmorphia works. It all starting this morning when I put on my
Victoria's Secret Pink leggings and set my right foot next to my
left. I could instantly feel it. My inner thighs were touching. My
eating disorder just told me to kill myself right there and then. I
almost did. It was official I was a "healthy," and there was not
enough will power to play nice today. Today My eating disorder
had the spotlight. No one was going to stop it. On top of how
horrible I was feeling this morning, I had to get ready for my
family meeting today. In the room with everyone this afternoon,
during my session, I couldn't fake my emotions. All I could do
was sit on the chair, tears running down my face super pissy. The

doctor was staring at me, and so was my family. I had nothing to say to this was the first time I let them see what raw emotions were on the inside of my base layer and what a mistake that was. The meeting ended with my doctor elongating my stay because of my behavior, followed by my mom saying she's not ready for me back at the house yet. Wow, way to make one feel rejected. I'm a discarded, immense waste of a human that gets to spend the rest of my summer while my friends are all building REAL memories. What a time to be alive right? I left the meeting, taking the remaining hours of my existence doing nothing piled up in a mess of anguish on my bed because I've followed the rules, and where did it get me? It got me stuck longer in the ward, wasting my summer. With that thought, I let my eyes roll to the back of my head, welcoming the darkness hoping that tomorrow will be better.

NEWBIES

Week three. The only time there are opportunities to look out for new tips and tricks is when new patients come to the ward, and we were just told by staff that someone new would be arriving this afternoon. I secretly wish the new person is bulimic or has another disorder because I can't bear to see anyone skinnier than me, sicker than me. I couldn't take another competitor at this weight, literally. Then I'm jolted out of my thoughts by the sound the 3 East B secured doors at the front. Those doors never open unless you're coming in or going out. The new kid must have just gotten here. My curiosity heightened. I started inching myself closer to the nurse's station. I managed to slither my way down the hall, pretending to go into my room for a better look. No chance. The kid (or so I'm assuming it's a kid) is already in their temporary place wailing hysterically. Poor thing. Reminds me of when I had my freak out at the EDIOP (eating disorder intensive outpatient program) with Liss and with Coet. I think our eating disorder patients have all had a meltdown before starting inpatient treatment. I believe that negative emotions would be expected, considering you're getting everything you have worked so hard for ripped from your hands.

It's been hours, and Clay, the newbie, is still all in a hysterical fit in his room. We were told by nurses today that the patient who had arrived this morning is a young boy anorexic, and we will be meeting him for the first time during lunch because he has agreed to participate. My blood drains — another anorexic. I'm well past the numbers I saw on the scale weeks ago, but finding out it's a boy made me feel more comfortable and very curious. So, lunchtime rolls around. I'm already impatiently waiting in my designated seat that sits around the dining table because I'm super interested in finding out who the new guy is. It looks like everyone else is absorbed too because they're all accounted for. All eyes peeled to the hallway that connects all the bedrooms. It takes a while for him to come out. I almost thought that we were going to start without him. I'm wrong. One of the LVN's escorts him out into the kitchen where we all are. Sniffling, he takes his spot right next to all of us. The first thing

I notice is the intense contrast between his features. His skin icy white and hair shoulder length, a dominant brown. His body, you could noticeably tell, was tiny even under all the baggy clothing he was wearing. His eyes were big and brown as well, and he looked so innocent. I felt poorly for him because he looked so young. Having an eating disorder mindset at such a young age is heartbreaking. To think in perspective to lose the pleasure of waking up in the morning because of the depressive thoughts and going to bed at night knowing that you probably won't sleep. Losing the joy of social gatherings because all you're thinking about is what you can and cannot eat. Your starving body distracted by food. To become uninteresting as a person so fast because of this malady. To become uninterested in things where you once had a passion. Our eating disorders took away the things that we enjoyed because it wants the limelight. You let your sickness have it, and now you have a new identity. You now carry the burden of an obsession with food and massive hate for it and the same time. That's when I truly lost myself. I forgot who I was becoming; I just let my disease take over.

I'm brought back at the moment when lunch starts. I have to annihilate a massive meal in half an hour. I let out a big breath to prepare my body for the torture I'm about to put it through. On the menu today is a ham sandwich with lettuce, tomato, and white bread. A green salad, fruit, an apple juice, silk vanilla soy milk, a packet of yellow mustard, a bundle of mayonnaise, chips, and a chocolate chip cookie in plastic wrap to top it off. I have to eat everything. I strategically plan out what I was going to eat and how I was going to eat it in order. I'm getting pretty good at hiding things at this point, but I am always on the lookout for new tricks. I glance around and see that Clay hasn't touched anything at all. Hm, so we have a protester here another Lara, perhaps? He shyly starts to speak to the nurse. His voice is so soft I can barely hear it, but I do. He asks for pancakes. What? Pancakes? I'm confused. He's so small, yet here he is asking for one of the significant fear food list items, I am lost.

The nurse then turns him down of his request and carry on to try and get him to eat some of the lunch items on his tray. He starts to fire back with questions and concerns about why he couldn't just get some pancakes. That spiraled into more no's from the nurses and a tantrum from the once shy cute little boy. As I manage to finish my last forkful, I look around. Most everyone at the table has either cleared and left for the Dayroom. Or they are about to end — all except one patient, Clay. Even Lara has eaten everything on her plate and has moved towards the Dayroom.

The staff keeps on trying to persuade Clay to have some of his lunch and talk to him gently about other subjects to keep his mind distracted, but it isn't working; he's still in hysterics. They always go easy on the first meal for new patients. I'm assuming that he'll get let off this time. To my surprise, they give him not one, but two ensures. He chugs them down. I think everyone is confused about this one, but each eating disorder is unique, so you can't judge. You can only sit back and watch. That's precisely what I decided to do. Sit back and perceive him.

Thinking about my personal task at hand, an elderly group of people starts to flood in the kitchen, and they have dogs! This morning in group check-in, Sussy told us that we were going to have animal therapy today. All the patients were informed and had been expecting it. What I didn't expect was the fact that I'm drawn to the cute little fluffy scraps. I don't usually care that much for dogs because I've always been a cat person. No lie. It was given to me by my family. My dad, mom, grandma, aunt, anyone in the family would give me cards with kittens, TY beanie babies that were cats, notebooks, you name it. My sister (who is one and a half years let than me) got everything dog. So there you have it.

I was ingrained to be a cat person. It was nice that the group of people that came in were elderly. I would've had anxiety if they were closer to our age. I carefully crept down to pet one of the dog's ears. It swiftly swung its head around to lick my hand. I let him have a go on my salty skin. After the pup had enough, I wiped the froth on his coat then headed towards my bedroom to wash my hands and have a bit of quiet time. I needed space and sleep. Recovering the nutrients your body needs takes a lot out of you.

Dinner was impending when I awoke from my nap. Perfect just in time to catch up on my observations on Clay. I ran to my spot at the dining table and waited, waited some more, and waited for what seemed like forever until everyone grabbed their positions next to me. Clay was last to his seat next to Lara, of course, and as soon as we were all properly seated, Bary, the LVN who decided to sit with us, started the ED dinner clock. 30 min, let's go. Tonight's spread was spaghetti Bolognese with a giant piece of garlic bread, one greasy pat butter, a green salad with thick creamy opaque ranch dressing, and as always vanilla soy milk with an apple juice. Not the worst that I've ever had, but that must mean I'm approaching a maintenance weight meal plan.

Panic starts to set in. Sharp tears form in the corner of my eyes. My nose starts to burn a little. I never planned on being this weight again. I have tried with all the willpower I have to avoid this at all costs. Now sitting here fighting with what's healthy for me and my old habits, I am torn. I'm trying to be ok with the feeling of my flesh stretched out and filled in. I'm trying to be ok with the roundness of my womanly body. I'm trying to be ok with the curves it's supposed to have, but I can't. I can't be ok with my thighs touching and the heavy feeling of only walking around. It's too hard not to hear all the negative voices that consume my mind. A tear falls to the ground as I shovel a forkful of spaghetti in my mouth. I don't wipe it away. I hope the trail it left behind on my cheek dries as I try and hide the personal battle I'm currently experiencing.

I look at Clay for a distraction and notice that he's not having the most considerable time over the dinner menu. He's having a fit of not having any breakfast foods again and acting as he did at lunch earlier. I watch as the nurses prepare the ensure plus in a Styrofoam cup and place it in front of him, stripping away any belief that he is going to touch his meal. The final minutes pass at dinner. Again, Clay is the last standing candidate. He's not even allowed to drink the medicine like dense drink until the allotted time is over. He ingurgitates the chalky substance so fast and scurries towards the hallway back to the rooms. Nurses charge after him because of the line of sight rule, and they probably think he's going to go vomit, but it's just another episode of hysterics this time.

EATING DISORDERS ANONYMOUS

It's always visiting after dinner then a process group, but today after visiting hour wrapped up, we were instructed to line up and follow the nurses to the downstairs conference hall for an open group. I felt goosebumps welt up on my arm as we walked down the hallway leading towards the main conference room.

I was nervous because I didn't know what to expect. There could be a very judgmental kind of anorexics that will judge me think that I'm not "sick" enough to be in inpatient because I don't think I am. My insecurities holding me back from experiences is something I am used to, it's something I am cursed with. However, I was interested in what others had to say. Maybe in hopes of discovering a cure of my own to help myself. Plus, I had to go. It was mandatory for ED patients on higher levels to attend. My eating disorder tagged along too. It comes everywhere with me. Nothing new. It only came to pick up on the unique rituals and habits. It'll probably get a few knowing that the other eating disordered people that have decided to go to this group will accidentally spill information when sharing their own stories of grief.

We enter the conference room we're a group of people are sitting in chairs formed in a circle in the middle of the room. There's a blank set of chairs in a row. I count the seats to reassure myself that's where we will be. I'm right. We are ushered over to the empty row. One by one, we sit in our spots with our parents while Dr. A, who is leading the group, explains who we are. I secretly thank him because we all need an excuse for looking indecent. We all take our spots, each one of us facing strangers. Each one of us vulnerable, anxiety-ridden, and suffocated with the thought of letting go.

Dr. A broke the awkward silence way too noticeable for the supportive crowd, aka parents and supporters. He started by introducing himself to the group explaining that this would be an open group. The floor is free to anyone who would like to talk. He asked for there to be no triggers as in numbers, weight, calories. Everything else is fair game. He pointed to the right and set off a chain reaction of everyone saying their names and introducing themselves. It took quite a long time to reach around the whole circle because there were so many people, the group only happens once a month so it can get pretty packed. The room was so silent for the number of mouths that were present. Everyone's minds were probably racing like mine, but no one was moving their lips. Just then, a severely underweight woman asked about exercise in recovery. She looked so thin was the first thought that went through my mind. In this disorder, you're obsessed with comparing your size to others and continuously body checking. I was so infatuated with the way she looked I hardly heard what she said until someone else chimed in on her commentary and brought me back from my little zone out.

"Exercise in recovery is something we try and avoid" Dr. A was speaking up again. You could tell he wanted to change topics after he had been on the subject for so long. He redirected the group conversation to something else. I tuned out for the rest of the meeting. When it was over, we said goodbye to our parents. Hopefully, leaving them with a better insight into how the eating disorder brain works, we headed back to the adolescent ward. I lie down on my bed, trying to repeat the meeting. I'm trying to dissect the conversations that went on. I'm trying to gain perspective of a healthier life. I'm getting so tired of the routine. Someone save me.

TIRED

My eyes open. I am already sweating with massive amounts of anxiety. My thoughts from last night swarm and attack me as I lie still waiting for the sun to cascade over my cotton white sheets. I've put on weight. I feel broken. I sit and question the purpose of happiness. I wonder if there's such a thing as consistent happiness, but I know there's not. I start thinking back a couple of days ago when I blankly stared at myself naked in front of the extemporary aluminum metal mirror that's bolted in the bathroom. I almost shatter when I think about that moment when my eyes met the distorted reflection staring back. I feel as if I could have a breakdown. I manage to get away with gritting my frists till my nailbeds dig into my palms, and the flesh bleeds. I finally get up. I skip going to the bathroom for fear of the shameful emotional baggage. Wiping away the blood residue on my palm, I walk to the nurse's station to retrieve my tub full of toiletries and other grooming necessities. When I get back to my room, I get ready, staring at the floor. I despise every inch of myself. It is so much easier to avoid the situation then handle the reality of it. After doing the best I can with my appearance without looking any reflection of myself, I make my way to the Dayroom and kitchen. Eager to take my mind off my own life, so I don't dwell on things. I can't change; I switch my focus to my other senses. I inhale deep and the smell of our breakfast salvers. My stomach gurgles with a response to the intoxicating smell. I might be hungry for a change. My eating disorder immediately denies that fact and dismisses it completely. So, I let my stomach rumble trying to let the pain feel good. Trying to convince me that beauty is pain and self-torture is a small price to live with if you so happened to be brought up broken. When I glance up, I see the nurse has already checked and handed out the platters. I lift the lid to see what surprise is waiting for me on the other side, hoping that Winter had magically dropped my increase. She didn't. Today's breakfast is a whopping buttery double stack of steaming hot pancakes with syrup on the side. I ignore that detail for now. I can't dare to think about the dark maple sugary substance. I would rather see fruit. "No, you would rather see nothing" my eating disorder corrects me. I silently wish I wasn't as greedy enough to have even wished for anything else. Next to the stack of cakes is malleable looking scrambled eggs and two sausages burnt to a crisp. Thinking this is already going to be hard enough, I cringe when I find out I have not one but two pats of butter sitting on the side along with apple juice, soy milk, and a chocolate chip cookie. Groaning, I start because I want to have enough time to finish. Looking around at the other patients is about the only thing that is going to save me during this meal, and that's when I notice that Nic is a handful for a handful. Shoveling mounds of food into his mouth. He looks like a greedy child that has never eaten, insatiable. I didn't realize I was staring until a piece of buttermilk pancake fell off my fork. However, Nic didn't just grab my attention; everyone was staring. All-day yesterday this kid is throwing a fit screaming and crying, not letting a single morsel of food get past his lips and now this? He finished everything in 5 minutes. The mystery with this one continues. So does the never-ending long process of finding every single one of us a cure. My pancakes that were once almost palatable have completely lost their appeal. They have turned into a cold, wet rubbery waste of matter that I somehow have to transport from the table to my stomach. My eyes twitch fast as I scan the room in search of anyone disposing of their meal. Jackpot I spot Samm

pressing the backside of her plastic fork onto her tiny cut-up
pancake pieces and follow suit, but right before I am about to
send the fork plummeting down, I stop myself. I hesitate and
think to myself, what's the point. I don't hide my food this meal;
I do not know what stopped me all of a sudden. Perhaps I was
just lazy and tired, so tired of the never-ending tournament.
Whatever it was that stopped me, this could be the start of
something better than the skeletal life. Could you imagine? A life
where you're a little bit more carefree, where you can step
outside the house after eating maybe a scrap too much instead of
not going anywhere for days on end because of the "bloat." A life
where you could enjoy social gatherings. You're not lying to
every person you meet because your little white lie has turned
into a web of lies that make you exhausted. Tired of trying to
keep up with yourself constantly. My thoughts stop, I shovel the
remaining food onto my fork and down my throat so
mechanically that I hardly notice it all go down. The sludge sits
there heavily in my stomach, awaiting the acid to churn it into
waste. I want the feeling to go away. It doesn't. Guilt was all I
felt as I slumped over to a couch in the Dayroom. I curled up into
a ball to ease the pain of the last 45 minutes. The rest of the day

was a blur, as all I could think about was the tightness of my stomach. The acid is creeping up my throat. I was physically there but mentally broken. They finally got me, at least for today. The night started to fall. Stars appeared in the sky as we huddled around in a circle on the floor for night check-in. Since I have been complying, I petitioned for level 3, the highest level at Alta Bates. The one right before discharge. I sit there, concentrating on the other patient's wrap up. I'm sweating bullets from my palms, awaiting the final results my treatment team has planned for me. When you petition for a higher level as I had done, you have to make a speech as to why you think you're ready to move up, and I tried to dazzle them. It's not just the staff you to impress either the patients get to vote as well. Thank God I've befriended most of them, and I am certainly not cross with anyone. Of course, that's not the final say everyone obviously wanted me to go up a level (all of the patients want to see everyone doing better, we all secretly want to be the sickest) they weren't the audience I had to swoon it was my treatment team. Just then, Glory, the night nurse congratulated me as my treatment team has accepted my request. Just like that, I am now level 3. My mind starts racing about what Winter and Dr. A have been discussing. Panic stokes my insides as my eating disorder tells me how grotesque I am and not a liability anymore for them. I'm not sick enough anymore. They know my mind isn't healthy, but they need beds for those who are physically weaker than me. Those who still have the perfect amount of space between each inner thigh, whose veins protrude a seafoam blue through their translucent ghostly skin. It all feels disheartening. I'm still so sick in the head.

UNCOMFORTABLE

Morning came soon. When I tried opening my eyes, the crust that formed around my eyelids during the night would not budge. The crust forcefully tried to make my eyes remain the way they once were, shut. I scratched at them until I could blurry see the cold linoleum and thin white linen that is supposed to provide warmth while at rest. I can only get rest from medication nowadays. I used to shiver. Now I can't stop sweating. Night sweats mean my body is recovering. I guess that's what a proper metabolism does, though, doesn't it? It's supposed to keep your body warm mine is just on hyperdrive now that I've reached a "healthy" weight.

Part of me shutters as that thought processes resonate with me, repeatedly echoing, causing me to go insane for a slight moment. I managed to quickly shut that thought out to focus on the main goal, I.e., getting out of here. I maintained the rest of the

morning in a haze. I need to write down a to-do list and regime
for when I am back home. I need to play it safe until at least a
month has passed after discharge. I need to comply fully with a
smile overemphasized on my face causing unwanted wrinkles
because it's all for a show. I feel nothing but anger now, all I see
is red. All they see is happy to a successful recovery. Unless my
dumb emotional uncontrollable self slips like at my family
meeting, I harshly remind myself. All I can hear is ticking, the
ticking from the constant clock that runs 24 hours in my
subconscious. The clock that won't stop until I'm finally out of
this mess. I've had all day to do anything I please. All I can do
now is wallow in my depression, and go through the motions
until I am discharged. It's approaching. I've talked to my doctor,
and I know it will be in the next few days. Last night I managed
to gain a level three in the ward, which means I am about to taste
freedom. Almost like plunging your spoon into the dessert you've
been waiting for since before your dinner has even had a chance
to salivate your mouth. There are still some unnecessary
necessary motions to deal with to get through this game.
Ironically, dessert is one of them. I have had too much already. I
know I have to continue because I now know what to expect if

you emotionally breakdown. We all know that was a mistake. Decompressing in front of the ones you should trust. I ended up with more time, remember.

I drag myself to the bathroom and have my mini morning breakdown. I let the saltwater pour down my puffy cheeks and hit the floor violently. Then I cradle my noticeably heavy head in my hands. These are signs my body has filled up, become cosmic, and I am no longer thin. I cry even harder — ten minutes pass. I have managed to get myself together enough to start the day. As I walk out to the bedroom to get dressed, I step through the puddle of the pain of living my own life that came from my tears and let it soak into my feet. Every chance I get to look back upon the positive, my eating disorder creeps up on me and sends mounds of stress to me so that it can settle in and make me feel shit again. I can't stand it. I can't escape from it.

I feel like just a pond in their game of chess as they slide me around the chessboard only to be taken out by the opposite opponent, and I'm not their problem anymore. I'm now on level three you would think that would make me happy. You're wrong. It's the worst feeling. It's knowing you're closer to a healthy weight. It's knowing all the hard work that you have done on top of managing regular life, taken away from you. The last year pried from the grasp of your clenched fist within one month. You can never have what you want; people can only mold you. I feel like a problem that forcefully was made a lab rat for doctors and nurses to study. To better their practices and maybe to get an award at the end of the year. They only work for themselves at the end of the damn day.

I get dressed in the baggiest clothes I own to hide the now pronounced muffin top I've accumulated, the distended abdomen, the real me that isn't the real me I lie myself to be. I collect my packet filled with all the phycological educational carp I will burn when I discharge and head for the dining hall. I'm the one late today. I blame the puddle of saline still sitting on my bathroom floor. I take my seat and start shoveling. I don't try and hide food anymore; it's pointless. I don't look at anyone I just shovel and shovel and shovel. I'm drowning. There's no time to process anything. I lifelessly go through the motions. Breakfast, check, vitals, check, avoid my depression, unavoidable. Shit. Think about what's next on the schedule as an attempt to distract me. Something called DBT group for morning therapy? I catch myself becoming slightly interested, shocking. I can't keep up, but I can if they twist my arm. They have fragmented most of us thinking that we're doing something clinically productive. I don't have enough energy to ask myself if we are. I can feel my thighs chafing as I make my way to the group room. I disgust myself.

According to Phycology Today, "Dialectical behavior therapy (DBT) provides clients with new skills to manage painful emotions and decrease conflict in relationships. DBT specifically focuses on providing therapeutic skills in four key areas. First, mindfulness focuses on improving an individual's ability to accept and be present in the current moment. Second, distress tolerance is geared toward increasing a person's tolerance of negative emotion, rather than trying to escape from it. Third, emotion regulation covers strategies to manage and change intense emotions that are causing problems in a person's life. Fourth, interpersonal effectiveness consists of techniques that allow a person to communicate with others in a way that is assertive, maintains self-respect, and strengthens relationships."

Now, where have I seen this before? Oh, yea online. If you googled DBT therapy on your Mac at home because let's be real who owns a PC anymore, it states that DBT is for patients with borderline personality disorder behaviors. Excuse me, I may be an existential crisis at this moment of my life, but I am far from being bipolar. That's the sad part about being a lab rat in the inpatient hospital. You have to go through the same tests they put everyone through. I think it's lazy, but the medical field doesn't get paid enough, so part of me gets their process as well. I shuffle into the group room to gain an understanding of something I already want to avoid listening to. I'm practically the last one who sits down. The chair cushion crunches as it welcomes me. The new monumental version of me. I miss the days where the chairs wouldn't make a sound. I know it will just take time to get there again.

Time is always on my side. Time, the only thing I can count on, but what is time? Is it just us aging through sunrise and sunset until we dissolve? Is it a form of pressure that settles into our lives as soon as we create deadlines for ourselves? Is that what we learn in school? I can't remember. Just then, I catch myself staring at the little red hand on the clock. You know the one that's always moving quickly as if it's trying to run away from the fact that it doesn't get a break, it never stops moving. I see a little bit of humanity in that little sliver of a red hand and feel sorry for all of us. The lead therapist hands out a printed paper describing what DBT is. All I can think about is how many trees this place kills with the amount of printed, scanned, and copied pages of workbooks and literature they hand out to us daily. I skim through the page uninterested but slightly amused that some people have this disorder. It's interesting how the brain works. I continue to be coherent as the lesson goes by still and all, I'm still absent. Almost like a cat taking a cat nap, they never really entirely fall asleep. They are always alert because of predators, and the luring eyes of predators surround me. Before I know it, the group is over. I can go on existing in silence and aggressive verbal lashings from the inner radical that lives inside me. Since I am now a level up, and I'm at a BMI that is closer to my age, I get the privilege to accompany the rest of the almost graduated eating disorder patients down to the cafeteria. The point of this exercise is to get the patient ready to eyeball and scoop out their portions to meet the correct exchange amount that they are required to have for their dietary plan. I know. It sounds like a one percent problem. It sounds like a spoiled kid problem, attention-seeking problem, but it's all of those and none of those. All "the privileged" gather round the double doors that are automatically locked. My gaze shifts around. I realize that everyone looks like they've been sleeping for days: messy ponytails and old tees. I look down at myself. I seem to blend in. I look worse than I do when I'm dying with the flu on a regular day at home. I'm depressed. I can fake it with a smile and softness. I can't hide it on my appearance. That part now always shows through. I blame therapy. I stare at my reflection as we board the elevator to the cafeteria. I try to convince myself that the person staring back is not me to get through the afternoon. This act goes on until my insurance runs out. This act hides the emotional turmoil I am going through on the inside so I can survive. We're all just trying to survive. To graduate. To relapse.

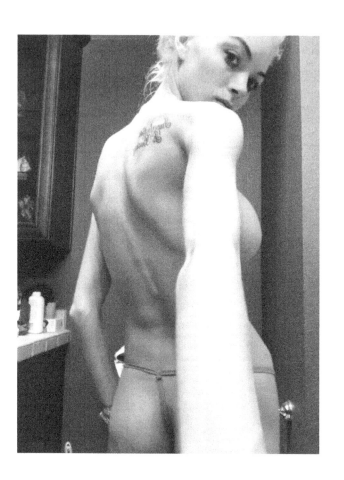

EPILOGUE

I don't want people to treat me like I'm fine and everything is ok because I look ok. That's the disease. I'm not fine, and I have been screaming for things to be better and change through the tops of my lungs. When that didn't work, I abused my body. When my body crumbled and almost left the earth, I was sent away to gain weight and look better. I was force-fed in inpatient and discharged. At a healthy weight, everyone thought I was fine again, but I was still not functioning mentally. No one cared to listen; they thought circumstances were better because I physically looked better. The abuse of my body started again.

A relapse struck harder than previously. That has happened multiple times throughout my adolescence into adulthood. I'm tired. I don't want this. Who would? I'm still not better, but I know I am the only one that can help myself at this point. The will to live is slowly fading. I'm just so tired. I ask myself, how are you managing things? Is it with your head out the outside of your stepfather's corvette vomiting from one to many glasses of wine driving back from a family dinner that was only 10 minutes away? Is it still hating yourself each moment the sun cascades through your blinds, waking you up? Damn, I still need to get those blackout curtains. I look healthy now, so everyone thinks I'm "fixed," but the truth is I am way more broken than I originally was. A new routine mildly crept into my life to help manage the weight gain. I'm still waking up to a soaked pillow from the previous night's uncontrollable sobbing. Depression holds me tight against the new linen my mom bought me to cheer me up. God bless her, but it doesn't help. The only thing that does is knowing that there's a hit of weed waiting for me in the garage. I roll over out of bed, tangled. In the same clothes from yesterday because I don't even bother to change that much anymore. Everything seems more of an effort.

My eating disorder is still there, camouflaging itself with other addictions. Molding, changing forum like a chameleon until one day when the Anorexia thinks it's safe to strike and take me down again, she will. She will only viciously attack when she knows everyone has turned a blind eye, and at that moment, I think my pathetic existence would be much more vastly simple if everyone were blind. I start towards the garage dragging myself using every last bit of motivation for life until I can finally take that hit of weed and heightened suggestibility clouds my thoughts. I can exist. My footsteps once dainty is now obnoxious and cause a disturbance to the calmness of my wants. I try to block out the carnage that overpowers my once positive thoughts, but all there is now is negativity. All the cognitive behavioral therapy I learned in inpatient walked right out the door with me when I was discharged. Why can't I be kind to myself? I stumble into the garage and head towards the cabinet where my stepdad stores his weed, but it's not there. Shit. I've been smoking so much he's been hiding it in different places, so I don't drag it all. Fair enough, my friends nicknamed me baby snake because they know I will keep going and going until the stash is dry like how baby rattlesnakes don't know how to control their venom well that's me. The me the doctors tried to change and failed. I finally find some grass. I load my bowl and light my lighter grazing the bud carefully not to burn the whole bowl in one go. What do you know? I guess I have learned a bit of delicacy? I take the last hit, and a wave of calmness settles. My mind is free.

Made in the USA
Middletown, DE
16 February 2021

33846720R00109